Leaning Forward

Toward Success

Leaning Forward

Toward Success

WHAT WE WEREN'T

TAUGHT IN SCHOOL

First Edition

Sean J. Harris

A LIONHEART MOTIVATIONS BOOK
Published by Thousand-Fold Publishing

Snellville, Georgia

Leaning Forward Towards Success

By Sean J. Harris

Published by
Thousand-Fold Publishing
P. O. Box 391416
Snellville, GA 30039
877-876-4529

To Order
http://stores.lulu.com/thousandfoldpublishing
Or email to:
thousandfold@bellsouth.net

ISBN-13: 978-0-6151-9325-0

Cover Design by
Victor R. Scott

Printed in the United States of America

Acknowledgements

A very special thanks go to my beautiful wife Janel. Your love and spirit gives me a daily reminder of the first day that we met. I love you and I'm very grateful for you always supporting me in every endeavor that I pursue. Dad, Mom, Sammy and Mayumi, I thank you all for completing me as an ambassador for success. Dad, thanks for letting me know that a book lived within me. To my business coaches, a WestPoint graduate and a prominent attorney by profession, I'm very thankful for the two of you becoming very instrumental in many of our successes. Thank you for your mentorship, leadership and friendship. Thank you to the entire Scott Family for their part in making this book possible.

Table of Contents

Introduction

What we weren't taught in school

Does this phrase sound familiar, "Go to school, get good grades and you will get a good JOB?" Well, it sounds as though we were all brought up in the same house right? Growing up, we were all led to believe that this was the proven path to success. As we have shifted from the Industrial Age into the Super Information Highway Age, we have witnessed many people on the side of the road as roadkill. This is due mainly in part from holding on to outdated thought processes.

As I grew and advanced in my entrepreneurial pursuits, I quickly learned that there were three types of education. The first form of education is an academic or scholastic education. This is where we learn the fundamentals of basic reading, writing and arithmetic. I was a "C" student throughout my school years. I just wanted to "C" my way out the front door to never return. I didn't have a high interest level when it came to sitting in a traditional classroom reviewing boring and unchallenging curriculum. I had a difficult time correlating how the academia we were being taught would relate to creating wealth in the future. I often tell people that I had an 11.25 GPA. At 11:25am, the lunch bell would ring. I majored in lunch and minored in Physical Ed. Later in life, I have come to recognize that many "A" students, teach "B" students, who many times find themselves working for the "C" student who usually owns the company.

The second form of education is what is known as a professional education. This form of education allows for us to specialize and enter a profession where we will receive income in exchange for working. The professional typically works for someone else, or is self employed; and likely attains a middle class lifestyle. As we know, with outsourcing and downsizing, the middle class is quickly disappearing. The third form of education is what is referred to as business ownership or financial education. This form of education teaches us how to leverage money. This will allow us to have money chase us rather than us chasing it.

Many of us learned to sell our time at a job in exchange for our wages. One could misplace a $20.00 bill. That $20.00 bill could be replaced, however, we can never remanufacture time. Once time is spent, it can never be replaced. Therefore, our time is more valuable than money. Sadly most people exchange time for money. Something of higher value for something of lower value. That is the same as trading a Ferrari for a Pinto! That just does not pass the common sense test. Why do we continue living this insane way of life? Doing today, what we did yesterday, thinking tomorrow is going to be any different.

In my youth, my father worked for a major copier company. I watched as he burned the candle at both ends as he built his own business in the copier industry. My mother was a cosmetologist. I would often see her invite side customers and clients to our home on weekends and evenings to earn additional income outside of the salon. Both my older brother and younger sister would sell candy and other goodies from their lockers and backpacks at school. I had always had visions of building a large business. I had always envisioned myself as the one calling the shots and not answering to a boss. So as you can tell, I come from a family filled with the Entrepreneurial Spirit.

Most guys get the infamous talk when they reach 17 or 18 years old. "Son, you have three options. You can either go to college, develop a trade or go to the military." Remember, school and I were not seeing eye to eye; I did not want a job because I did not like receiving instructions from a boss. So I decided to go to the United States Air Force. I thoroughly enjoyed my service to my country.

I have a background in Aeronautics/Aerospace Propulsion. Pretty good for a kid that just wanted to "C" his way out of school right? I recall being e-blank no-rank arriving at my first duty station. A well-dressed, highly decorated officer approached me and said, "Son, one day when you have been in the Air Force for 33 years, you can become a commander of a base just like I did." I was somewhat impressed until he turned to get into his car that was barely held together with Air Force Aim High bumper stickers. Now understand this, I was not the sharpest knife in the drawer, but I was not a butter knife either. I recognized that if after 33 years of doing something to create income, and that vehicle was the best he could do, I knew that that method of creating income did not work.

I exited the United States Air Force decorated and with an Honorable Discharge. I entered the field of Law Enforcement. I spent nearly eight years dodging bullets and kicking in doors for a living. This was fun and exciting. This way of creating income was based on my physical ability to perform, just as 98% of most people's jobs are based on their physical ability to perform. In your vehicle's trunk or under carriage, there should be a spare tire there. The purpose of that spare is "just in case". We must ask ourselves, "Do I have a spare income?"

I knew that I had to find another source of income in the event that I became incapacitated for an extended period of time.

More importantly, I examined the "X-out" factor. If you were "X'ed" out of the equation, what would happen to your family financially? I began researching information as it related to building my own company. While my co-workers and friends would waste their non-productive time doing non-productive things, I would use that same time engaging in productive activities. I built a company in the Real Estate industry while still maintaining my full time job in law enforcement. I later started a second business as a subsidiary company of the first one.

My income quickly matched and soon surpassed my job income. I was excited and things were going great. After becoming debt-free, I was able to leave my full time job to continue growing my new businesses. Within that same year, my wife Janel and I started a Business Development Firm, which has today grown into a successful International Company. We've expanded throughout the U.S. and other countries. Janel and I speak today at many seminars and other events.

If you are seeking information on starting your own business, excelling in the corporate world, developing leadership or becoming a team player, this book will give you a tremendous foundation in which to build from. Whether you are an entrepreneur, athlete, pastor, student, or coach; you will have the opportunity to peek into the mind and thought processes of successful business builders. This book is designed to add value to your life. Tools make a task easier, take this tool and put it to work in your life!

Continuously Prospering,

Sean J. Harris

Leaning Forward

Toward Success

While formal schooling is an important advantage, it is not a guarantee of success nor is its absence, a fatal handicap.

– Ray Kroc

> **Planning is bringing the future into the present so that you can do something about it now**
>
> *Alan Lakein*

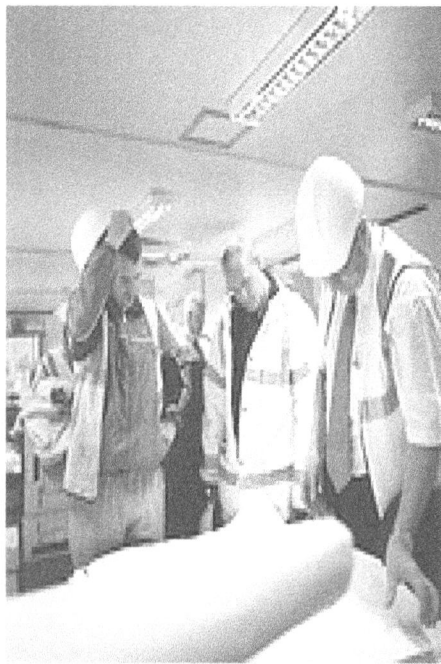

Chapter I

Plan Your Plan and Work Your Plan

THERE ARE TWO PRIMARY REASONS PEOPLE BECOME frustrated when it comes to achievement. Many people either do not have a plan or they have a plan, however are not working that plan. Sound familiar to anyone? Unequivocally, these two have been identified as the two major challenges that cause the most aggravation to those seeking success. This in turn causes many people to become paralyzed in their actions due in part to uncertainty.

Have you ever entered a beautifully decorated spacious home that was so picturesque? Remember commenting on that twelve-inch crown molding, the stunning hardwood floors, with

Italian marble countertops. Wasn't it amazing how much of God's nature could be viewed from that oversized palladium window overlooking a lightly wooded backyard. How about that humungous kitchen with two sub-zero refrigerators. How about a twelve-foot island with a built in aquarium underneath with a three-foot bullshark swimming around? Guys we all love that finished lower level that we all desire. There is the surround-sound system, the theatre, fitness room and sauna. Let's take a moment here. At any point did we make mention of that stunning, incredible, most attractive part of the house? The foundation. That's right, the foundation.

We never go into a home and say in amazement, "Bob; this is the best looking foundation that I have ever laid my eyes on!" Well, the foundation is the most unattractive, time consuming, expensive and unseen portion of the house. However, it is the most important part of the building process. The potential size of the house that can be built is directly correlated to the size and structure of the foundation.

There must be a plan identified to build a home or building. Architects use blueprints in planning the building of an edifice. The same holds true for building your dreams and future. Most people who don't achieve their dreams did not plan to fail, they just fail to plan. But recognize, failure is not failure unless you quit. Success is built from repeated failures. The most successful person is the person who failed the most.

In the Air Force we used a process referred to as backwards planning. In order to plan we must know and understand our objective. My business mentor, would always teach me that, "we must begin with the end in mind".

If my goal were to gain fifteen pounds of pure muscle mass, I would need to develop a gameplan. I must determine what my new eating regime would become. I would need to study which exercises would be sufficient to add the strength needed to lift the poundage that would lead to the muscle growth desired. I would then determine the number of sets and repetitions that would be required as well as the length of time required. Planning a trip to Disney

World© would utilize the same backwards planning just as planning your future.

It is a good idea to plan in three phases. We should set a three to six month plan, a one-year plan and a two to five year plan. Goal setting should be very similar. A short term, mid-term and long-term goal should be set. Everyone should have a business plan whether you own your own business or being a great employee or student. Success will not run you down and tackle you in the street and yell, "I'm all yours!" You have got to go get it. Reminds me of cruising to the Caribbean with my wife. We were lying on the beach of Cococay Island in the Bahamas, and out in the distance about two miles away awaited our cruiseliner. I remember over hearing a guy complaining to his wife that the cruiseliner should come in closer for boarding instead of having to take a four-minute ferry out to the ship. Well two thoughts came into my head. The first thought was that this guy obviously was never in the Navy. Secondly he did not understand that many times our ship has come in, but it's our responsibility to swim out to it. Many people are not willing to go meet their ships of success. All too often, great opportunities are not gift wrapped with a pretty little ribbon and bow around it.

Once you have written your plan out on paper, have it reviewed by your mentor. Oh yeah, I did say mentor. All successful people have mentors. We will discuss mentorship heavily in later chapters. Another "Golden Rule" that I learned while serving in the Air Force was that if it is not in writing, it does not exist.

You may say Sean, planning is not one of my strengths. That's totally ok. Start with daily planning. A technique that I personally find very helpful for me in regards to planning is the use of index cards. Each evening prior to going to sleep, I take an index card and write down everything that I must accomplish the following day. After each task is written down, I number each one in the order of priority. Now understand there is a difference between important and urgent. Whatever item is marked as number one represents the first task to be accomplished. I will write the time in which the activity is to start and the time of anticipated completion. This allows each item to be achieved fairly early in the day. Another axiom is to hurry up and wait. I am the type person that if you assign a task scheduled for completion in a week, I would have it completed by Wednesday and enjoy stress free time the remainder of the week.

Time management is definitely a topic we will discuss in further chapters. Time management is one of the keys to success. There are so many keys to success that you may sometimes feel like a janitor, however each individual key is a must to unlock the doors of success. If there are any items on my list that are not that pressing and could be completed by someone else, I will usually delegate those activities. Writing your daily activities allows you to remain accountable for your time. Remember, we all have the same allotted amount of time in a day and we can never get back the time once it is spent. Invest it well!

Many people spend more time planning their vacation or their child's birthday party than they do in planning their own futures. Take a few moments and dream about what your ideal life would be like if you had no time or financial restraints. We will come back to that thought in one second. If I were to walk down to my neighborhood park and find any six-year-old boy, I could ask him what is it he would like to do or become, as he grows older. Without hesitation, he would rattle off every profession under the stars. He would like to be a doctor, a police officer, a firefighter, an astronaut, a basketball player, and a football player. He would then gasp for air and continue with his dreams and aspirations of becoming the President of The United States and so on. It is only when the child is told to quit dreaming, does he begins to lose his vision. He is told you cannot possibly do all those things. Maybe not, but he can focus and do any one or two of those things. I managed to become a police officer, a deputy sheriff, an aerospace propulsion specialist, built two companies in the real estate field and launched a successful international company before the age of twenty-eight. As

> "What would you do with no restraints on your time or finances?"

the saying goes, whatever the mind can conceive and believe, it will achieve!

Going back to the question I just asked regarding what would you do with no restraints on your time or finances. What would be your plan for your tomorrow, next week, next year, your life? Once you visualize you dream in your mind's eye, develop a plan by using the backwards-planning technique to achieve it.

Growing up in my family, we did something that I believe is an unheard of in today's times. We would have weekly family meetings. On a weekly basis my parents would gather my brother, sister and I to sit in the den area. We would discuss family events and talk about things pertaining to the well being of the family. We talked about our individual plans and linked all of our plans into one family plan. I would strongly recommend taking the time to meet with your family and discuss goals and plans for your family. This is a great opportunity to teach your children the things important to you that you would rather teach than to rely on the school system or peers to teach them. This is the window of opportunity to connect with and get to know your children even better allowing you to be informed on what is going on in their lives. Develop your plan, and work your plan diligently.

Faith is taking the first step even when you don't see the whole staircase.

— Martin Luther King, Jr.

Exercise to stimulate, not to annihilate. The world wasn't formed in a day, and neither were we. Set small goals and build upon them.

— Lee Haney

Opportunity dances with those already on the dance floor.

H. Jackson Brown Jr.

Chapter II

The Importance of Dress and Appearance

MONDAY MORNING AT 9:07AM, YOU RUSH FRANTICALLY into the board room with five of your industry's top professionals awaiting your 9:00am presentation on time management of all topics. This was a do or die presentation for you to be considered to join the executive team. As you enter the room for introductions, you as well as the executive team notices the smudge on your shirtsleeve, your oversight of your five o'clock shadow forming before brunch and the fruit preserves stain on what was your favorite necktie. Can you say Calgon© take me away? You guessed it. You blew it with a capital "B". First impressions do not get a second opportunity. This is a topic that we will dive deep into through out this chapter. A book should be dedicated to this subject alone. Well, let's see how well we can compress a book into a chapter.

We have all heard the expression, Dress for Success. This is a must to achieve ultimate success. I will cover men's dress and appearance and my wife Janel will include valuable details on women's dress and appearance. Let's get started men beginning from head to toe shall we?

Hair. To some extent in the business world, hairstyles can make or break you. There is an important difference between professionalism and fads. Please understand the difference. It probably would not be a good idea to offer a presentation with a Mr. T. Mohawk. Even though this was a cool hairstyle in the 80's, it is not on the top ten list in the new millennium. Here's a good rule of thumb to go by for acceptable hairstyle. Look in professional publications and periodicals and observe the type styles that are favored for your particular industry. Hair should not touch or

> # First impressions do not get a second opportunity

hang over your ears or shirt collar. Sideburns if worn, should not extend below the lowest point of the opening of the ear canal. Avoid using excessive hair care products. A great litmus test here is to observe your headrest in your vehicle. If there is residue, this is an indication that you may be using too much hair care products in your hair. Look sleek, not slick. Women's hair should be very tasteful. Women have the luxury of variety when it comes to hairstyles. Extravagant colors would not be an ideal choice for a professional image. Well trimmed hair portray a successful confident image.

Many professionals will agree that the less facial hair men have, the more people tend to trust and have confidence in them. Think back to the old western movies. Who had stubble and who had the clean-shaven face? The same is true for modern movies. Many men may say, "my mustache makes me look older, or my wife likes it". Well, I have learned first hand from the top business leaders in this country, that 4oz of hair could hold you back from many opportunities.

Now I understand for many religious beliefs, facial hair is tradition. I am not referring to those beliefs. If facial hair is a must for you, keep it well groomed and maintained. However, ensure that people around you cannot tell what you had for lunch two hours later because of the residual hung up in your mustache. Mustache wearers, the corner of your mouth should be the gauging mark as to the extent of the width of your mustache. Also prevent hair overlay of the top lip.

Teeth are one of the first notable things people see in the first three seconds of meeting you. If you have dental challenges, take the time and money necessary to invest in corrective actions. This is one of the best personal investments a person can make. Have your teeth professionally cleaned routinely, especially if you are a smoker or coffee drinker.

Breath could be a huge barrier and turn off for people that you come in contact with. Breath strips and mints are a great asset and should be kept on your person at all times. We want people to focus on what we are saying and not the toxic fumes that sometimes exude from our mouth. We don't want them to revisit that triple stack onion burger that we had for lunch right? Nor do we want them to be torn between handing us a breath mint or a roll of toilet tissue.

> There is an important difference between professionalism and fads.

Manicures, Men as masculine as we all like to be and appear, many of us think manicures are not manly. Just the opposite is true. First it reveals that you have a good self image and are secure in who you are. Guys one of the first things most ladies focus in on is the care we put into our hygiene. Ladies like men with clean soft strong hands. Not hard callused rusty hands. Use lotions to keep moisture in your hands so that people won't feel as though they are shaking the hand of Mr. Sam Sandpaper. Keep your fingernails cleaned and trimmed.

Ladies, the care of your hands speaks volumes about you. Whether you wear long nails, short nails or artificial nails, you should keep them in good repair. Clear coat nail polish is always acceptable. French tip manicures gives a professional image. Tasteful red colors are feasible options. One of the most unattractive sights related to fingernails are nails displaying chipped polish. Even worse are broken rigged nails or artificial nails in bad need of a fill repair.

Jewelry, Avoid wearing excessive jewelry. The maximum amount of rings that men should wear is two. One should be your wedding band and some other tasteful ring such as a class ring or athletic ring. One ring per hand is a good rule of thumb. As with men, excessive jewelry is not acceptable in the professional arena. Your jewelry should be in good taste. Women, rings on every finger definitely does not shout professional image. It's not the best idea to go overboard with earrings extending from the top of your earlobe to the bottom. In a professional setting, you may want to refrain from oversized earrings. Multiple bracelets could also be viewed as excessive. A nice tennis bracelet or ankle bracelet serves as a nice accent piece.

Makeup – makeup should be applied in tasteful moderation. We wouldn't want to look like the local clown at the city circus would we? There are several creative things that can be done involving makeup. I recommend that good professional judgment be used here.

Watches, with business attire a watch with a metal or leather band should be worn. Watches with rubber bands should be reserved for the running track and the gym. This does not portray a professional image. A tasteful bracelet on the alternate wrist is acceptable.

Let's focus on attire. There are different categories of dress which we will identify each.

Shoes should be black or brown. Leather is always preferred in the business world. For men, lace-up shoes convey power and confidence. For women, flats or heels are commonplace in the business world. Shoe polish should be applied as well as heel dressing. Investing in a really nice expensive pair of dress shoes will reward you for years if properly cared for. Shoetrees are a great investment for ensuring the longevity of your shoes. It's always a great idea to purchase shoes with leather soles. Heels and soles can be replaced several times over the lifespan of your shoes. Wear dark dress socks, never white athletic socks.

Pants should be well fitting, clean and wrinkled-free. Slacks or Dockers are always a good choice for sharp casual dress. Trousers should be properly altered with relaxed fit in the seat and thigh areas. They should be hymned or cuffed. Cuffed trousers are more fashionable and current with the times. There should be one distinct crease down the center. Pleated pants add a pleasing and appealing look of distinction. If suspenders are worn, the number one fashion No-No is to not wear them with a belt! It's one or the other, never both. Wear the suspenders in a manner in which the pants will break nicely over the shoe. You wouldn't want to give the appearance you're out shrimping. Belts should be leather, black or brown. The buckle should be tasteful and not overly sized. The same standards for fit and alterations apply for women pants.

Shirts should again be well fitting. Dress shirts should have a collar that is snuggly fit. You don't want a vise grip shirt at the same time you wouldn't want to give the appearance of a pencil neck with inches to spare. It is always a good idea to go to an alteration shop and have all of your measurements taken professionally. Keep these measurements saved for future purchasing. Long

> **Dress equal to the attendees or one notch above.**

sleeved dress shirts should extend the full length of your arm. The sleeve should not go beyond the wrist. You can never go wrong wearing a white dress shirt. Light blue shirts are also common for business dress. Blouses come in various styles. Many blouses can be coupled with a matching scarf or neckpiece.

Ties present a very powerful statement and say a lot about the person. Expressive individuals tend to wear cartoon ties. This is not ideal for business. Great colors that demand power and respect are red, blues and gold. Ties should be silk and not too busy to the eye. One on the most successful business owners in the world has taught me that the smaller you are, the sharper and more impressive your tie should be. Your tie should compliment the color of your suit and shirt. The Windsor knot is the preferred knot worn by most successful people. Clip-on ties do not exemplify professionalism. If you are not accustomed to tying a tie, get with your business coach. Ensure that your tie isn't too long or too short. It should come right at the level of your belt buckle. You wouldn't want it too short; this could make you look as if you're wearing a bib.

Sport coats should be properly fitting in the chest, arms and back areas. Dark colors are preferred. Coats should not have 50 buttons! Two or three buttons are sufficient. Either single or double breasted are acceptable. Elbow patches are out dated and should be avoided. Side bar gentlemen, when traveling in a car do not wear your coat. Hang it up on the coat hook in your vehicle. A most unpleasing sight is a professional man in a wrinkled coat!

Women business suits usually consist of either two or three pieces. The suit could be either a pantsuit or a skirt set. A good rule of thumb is to keep the hem line low and the neckline high. Hosiery should be worn whenever a skirt is worn. Hosiery should coincide with your skin shade as well as compliment your outfit.

Both men and women should wear non-offensive fragrances in moderation. People should not smell you before they see you. A higher quality fragrance last longer and doesn't require heavy applications.

Different categories of dress are business attire, sharp casual and resort casual. It is important to understand that no matter your age, business attire is the same. For a seasoned professional or the college student, business dress consists of a dark business suit. Black, blue or gray would be acceptable in any business setting. Whenever you are attending a business event such as a seminar, you should always dress in business attire. Dress equal to the attendees or one notch above. Sharp casual would consist of slacks or dockers with a collared shirt such as a golf shirt. Acceptable shoes could be dress or loafers. Resort casual consist of dockers shorts and golf shirt or linens. An acceptable shoe would be loafers or upscale sandals.

Well class it looks like we covered the full spectrum on dress and appearance. Let's move on to the next block of instruction.

Our time is a finite resource;
money is an infinite resource.
Know how to balance the two.

Sean J. Harris

Chapter III

Economic Power

ECONOMIC POWER IS ACHIEVED THROUGH BUSINESS ownership. So often society cry's that it's the fault of the politician in office that are solely responsible for healthcare, pensions and other responsibilities surrounding creating a living legacy for your family's future. If you are hopelessly depending on the government to empower you with economic power, you are being led down a delusional road of disappointment. So often our society has changed the price tags in the middle of the night and the whole world continues to buy it. Your power is birthed once you decide and act upon that decision to sit in the driver's seat of your financial vehicle.

In our history books and classes, we were led to believe that Christopher Columbus sailed to America, met with the natives, high-fived each other and grubbed on turkey! How misleading! What many are unaware of is the fact that Christopher Columbus and the crew of the Mayflower were businessmen. This country was founded on business ownership. The travelers on the Mayflower set up their businesses when they arrived. During the agricultural age, 98% of people were business owners with 2% as apprentice to become business owners. It's it an American tragedy that now 2% of people own there own business and 98% are employees! The reason an employee's name and company in which they are employed are plastered on their uniform shirt is in case they wander too far off their plantation. Did he say plantation!?! YES I DID! Understand slavery isn't a racial thing; it's a socio-economic thing.

> # Slavery isn't a racial thing; it's a socio-economic thing.

The worst thing next to being a slave in the freest country in the world is being a slave in the freest country in the world and remaining a slave by choice. You have no economic power when someone else controls your time and income. How do I know if I have economic power you may ask yourself? Well, if you sign your check on the rear only, you do not have economic power. When you sign your check on the front and the rear; you're in control of your time and income, thereby you have economic power.

> # You have no economic power when someone else controls your time and income.

The goal of an employee is to create a profit. The goal of a business that the employee works for is to create a profit. These goals are diametrically opposing one another. On the company's balance sheet, the employee's salary falls on the expense/liability column.

The goal of the company is to keep the profits up and the expenses down. In this instance, the company will pay the employee just enough so that they won't leave, however not enough to ever get ahead. See, at a company there is only one goal and dream. That goal and dream is that of the business owner. These goals could range from financial independence to an enhanced lifestyle. The goal of the business owner is to discipline the employees to fulfill his or her dream. Each person will be disciplined. You will either be disciplined to fulfill your dreams and goals, or you will be disciplined by someone else to fulfill the dreams and goals of that person. Either way, you will be disciplined and a dream will be fulfilled during your lifetime.

Sean do you not like jobs? Jobs are necessary for a short period of time for seed money. This seed money then should be invested into your own dream. Jobs are not designed to accomplish financial independence. Becoming a business owner will require you to burn the candle at both ends and maybe in the middle as well. This will not be required forever and at some point, sooner rather than

> **If you don't know the rules, you will never have the ball thrown to you**

later, you will be able to blow one end out. Business ownership brings out the champion in you. It affords you the opportunity to leave a legacy and set a great example of leadership to your children and their children. The premier business ownership manual that I read tells us that we are to bless our children's children. Business owners fuel the economy. We provide jobs and give others the opportunity to sustain a lifestyle. For those who have vision and focus, these individuals often move forward and afford others jobs through businesses that they create. Isn't it interesting that the age of many employees of fast food establishments are shifting from 16-18 years of age to the other end of the spectrum, 50-65+ years of age? These are all great people who didn't necessarily plan on being at that point in their lives, however they just failed to plan. So many people outlive their money. Recognize that our school system does not teach us how to own our own businesses. We are taught how to get good grades, work very hard for many years for someone else and everything should be happily ever after. Tragically, this fairytale turns into a nightmare for most people. We must first teach ourselves the different types of education. Once we've learned and master them ourselves, we must educate our children in these areas. There is an academic education, a professional education and financial education. If you don't speak the language of a foreign country that you are traveling to, you will have difficulty managing in that country. The same holds true if you are in the land of finances and you don't speak the language. How could you ever expect to live and prosper in this land without becoming fluent with the language and culture of finances? To become successful in business or anything else, a mentor is a must. We'll discuss this in future chapters. If you don't know the rules, you will never have the ball thrown to you. You can never expect to win any game without knowing the rules.

> **Becoming a business owner will require you to burn the candle at both ends**

Only the mediocre are always at their best

— Jean Giraudoux

I try to learn from the past, but I plan for the future by focusing exclusively on the present.

— Donald Trump

If you can keep playing tennis when somebody is shooting a gun down the street, that's concentration.

Serena Williams

Chapter IV

Distractions

THE SUMMER OF 1979, IN HOT ORLANDO FLORIDA, A 6 year old smiley faced child was enjoying himself at the world famous Disney World©. He had cotton candy in one hand and a toy in the other. Things couldn't be any better until his focus on fun turned into his fear of distraction. I was this kid. I was enjoying a family vacation with my parents, brother and newborn sister. I clearly recall standing near the Huck Finn paddleboat attraction. I spun myself dizzy frantically searching a 360° glance for my lost family members. Ok, I was the one lost. What was actual ten to fifteen minutes felt as if I were experiencing back to back eternities. Clearly I knew that I would never find my family members again amongst the thousands of strangers surrounding me. Surely, I would never enjoy my mom's banana pudding, fishing with my dad and brother. I would miss the joys of having a baby sister to pick on.

I remember being temporarily rescued by a little girl who must have been seven or eight years old accompanied with her mother. I had a display of Niagara Falls flowing down my terrified face from my swollen eyes. In my worst moment in my six years of existence, the little girl made the never-ending devastation even worse. She said, "Mommy, can we keep him?" As if I were a lost and found puppy. My crying increased in decibels, which I believe was the attributing factor that caused my parents to locate me. Needless to say, I had a vise grip hold on the handle of my sisters' stroller the remainder of the trip. From this point forward, I demonstrated pinpoint laser focus on the whereabouts of my family. This was my first experience in life with major distraction.

> ### Some distractions are blatant and others are discreet.

Life is and will be full of distractions. Some major and devastating, while others may be simple but annoying enough to get you off track from your focus. There are different forms of distractions that I will address throughout this chapter.

Some distractions are blatant and others are discreet. Some are self-imposed while others originate from external sources. They can consist of family, friends, jobs, business, health, finances, or the lost of a loved one. As uncomfortable as it is to accept, family can be one of the biggest distractions. Many people make decisions be it financial, business, or marital based on the approval of family members. To demonstrate leadership, a person must have the ability to be independent, while remaining interdependent. So often when people are striving forward toward a goal or objective, they at times lose focus due to comments or actions that a loved one may have said to distract or knock them off their track of success.

A prerequisite to becoming successful is to be an independent thinker. You must have the power of focus. A photographer focuses his camera to take a perfect picture. Now picture your future without focus. Doesn't look clear huh?

Don't be held back by the influences of other people who lack knowledge in your pursuits. When a person doesn't understand something you may be pursuing, they often perceive what you are doing is wrong. The average person can't explain or draw out the formula for the law of gravity. Regardless of whether you understand how gravity works or not, you believe it works. If you step out of a second story window, you would unequivocally prove the law of gravity true. Another tip to acquiring success is to recognize when we don't know or understand something. The second part to this is to be intelligent enough to associate with those who

> A person must have the ability to be independent, while remaining interdependent

can educate us in these areas beyond our understanding. Just because we are uninformed or unversed in a subject does not make the subject an untruth. Many times people we know will criticize projects we are pursuing. This comes as a result of our stepping out and shining our light on what they are not accomplishing. What a person hasn't experienced or been exposed to can be viewed as unproven or unbelievable. It's not a good idea to allow others to decide the road that you travel. You must be the one in the driver's seat of your financial vehicle. Friends can be another huge source of distractions. Our friends, especially life-long friends seem to know us better than we know ourselves. Actually no one knows you better than you do. When we haven't seen a friend for a while, they see you today as they saw you last.

Many of my Air Force buddies would remember me with my head in a toilet bowl at the NCO club if they see me today without having seen me since my military days. That's their last visual image.

Therefore it may seem difficult for some of them to believe that I'm the successful owner of three companies as well as an author.

Some "friends", (and I use that word loosely) who don't see themselves advancing in life will sometimes frown upon you excelling. You see, as I previously mentioned, when you move forward and shine, your light shines on their weaknesses, inadequacies and tasks that they aren't accomplishing. You can always determine your future and where you are going by looking at your top five friends. Your friends reflect your self-image. There are three things my business coach taught me must be changed in order to change my life.

The first area to evaluate was with whom I associated. Just as important as it is to associate with the right people, it is equally, if not more important, to disassociate with the wrong people. Associate with friends who are focused and success driven. I still have old friends, however the amount and type of time I may spend with them has significantly changed. You can either spend time with people or invest time in and with people. Friends are important, just ensure that they add value to you and you to them.

> **Your friends reflect your self-image**

The second area that must be evaluated were the books I read. I learned that your finances are directly related to the books you read.

The third area was to determine what I used my spare time doing. Since we all have the same allotment of time per day, no one should ever say that they don't have time. We must master the efficiency of the time that we have. To qualify my time, I ask myself, "will the activity I'm about to partake in yield an income and increase my net worth?" If the answer is no, then I re-evaluate if I should continue that particular activity.

Jobs can be an unpleasant distraction to your goals. Many success-seeking individuals are stifling their potential by being limited by what a job may offer. Jobs may offer either time or money but never both. There's only one dream at a job and it belongs to the owner. Think about it. Who works harder, you or your supervisor? Ok, who earns more money you or your supervisor? This is basically corporate prostitution. Is my point clear enough? Jobs are good for developing seed money to use in establishing your own personal goals and dreams.

Have you ever thought about owning your own business? I have known people who have launched their own businesses in conjunction to working their full time job. Unfortunately for some, just as their businesses began to take off, they would get a promotion at their job, which distracted them from building their own company. See many times you must be willing to give up something good to receive something great.

> "My Job, My Office or Our Projects." Unless your name is on the building, I don't think it's your job!

Today's society lives on immediate gratification versus delayed gratification. The promotion usually required longer hours, travel or relocation. I decreased my output in my real estate company drastically to put more time in my business development firm. My development firm is the company that sustains future generations for my family. You must know when to give up the carrot that your job daggles in front of you in exchange for the lobster and steak dinners that your own business can provide. By the way, in cartoons, what type of animal do you associate with that chased the carrot on a string at the tip of a stick? You said it, I only thought it.

Be thankful for your job, but don't rely on it long term. Recognize that if Bob has seniority at a company with twenty years under his belt, he is more dispensable than the two twenty year olds new to the work force. The company is lucky if Bob works a full eight-hour day. Bob receives full benefits and receives top salary.

The two twenty-year-old guys work eight hours a day each totaling sixteen hours of production for the company. Even though they may work full time hours, they are hired on as part-time workers. This allows the company to pay contractor type salaries and does not have to pay out medical and dental benefits. Because this is the young guys first real job, the company can manipulate them into working extra hours. The extra hours benefit the company and is an exploitation of the young guy's energy.

Just as your company loaned the position to you, surely they can take it back. Notice I said loaned. I often hear people say "My Job, My Office or Our Projects." Unless your name is on the building, I don't think it's your job!

Owning a business can be a distraction to your personal obligations, be it your family or any other areas of your life outside the business. Being successful will create the sense of being out of balance, however you must still have some sense of balance.

Health affects a large percent of our population as a distraction. Health challenges could be personal health or the health of a family member or close friend. With healthcare what it is today, many can't afford it. Poor health is not only a distraction to daily activities but usually brings about a screeching halt to all activities. Health is one of our most precious assets. The declining health of a loved one or ourselves, affects nearly every area of our lives. Poor health affects the clarity of our thoughts. Many times we only relate health to the physical aspect. We must also strengthen and maintain our mental and emotional health.

Financial responsibilities hinder our ability to focus on what really matters. Financial difficulties always lead to health challenges to some degree. A health challenge that most people can relate to is STRESS. Imagine waking up one morning knowing that you are debt free, in good health, with healthy relationships, and that money continues to flow into your ever growing bank account. Wouldn't this allow you to focus, eliminating most distractions? I've experienced all of the above listed distractions plus many others, as I'm sure you have too. It's how we handle them that are important. At one of the early peaks of success in building my business development firm, we received a diagnosis about my father's health. About one year later we received a similar diagnosis concerning my mother's health. This was a very difficult time in my life. Building a thriving company while maintaining focus on both parents health is a very difficult situation to have experienced. I had to wear the "everything is fine" hat as I gave seminars and lead business owners that I mentored. As leaders we don't have the luxury of having a bad day. Our lowest low must still be higher than the highest high of the people we lead. You can never achieve victory if you cannot move beyond your feelings.

We cannot direct the wind but we can adjust the sail

— Bertha Calloway

The more sand that has escaped
from the hourglass of our life, the
clearer we should see through it.

Jean Paul

Chapter V

The Hill To Success

Relying on a Job

| Rough cliff to climb with jagged edges. Many tools needed to climb. Plenty of stress on the body on this side. The top is not in sight. These are the effects of attempting to reach the top utilizing the job route. |

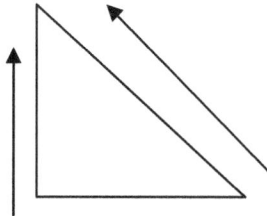

Having a Business

| Able to jog the slope gradually, controlled, consistently & persistently. Tools needed are comfortable jogging shoes & good attitude. Here you are strengthening the body & can see the top of hill. |

People often pray for opportunity. It would be more beneficial however to pray for recognition of opportunities. Opportunities surround us constantly. Unfortunately, many people have not been trained to recognize and identify them. Often we think that opportunities must be dressed up in a sharp business suit or a pretty box with a flowing red ribbon on it. Many times the opportunities that we are seeking are found in the center of adversity.

Opportunities are never lost; they are just passed on to someone else ready and prepared to recognize them. You can't be afraid and leery of taking calculated risks. Well Sean, how do I know when to take a risk? To take a risk doesn't have to be a difficult process. First, take a look at the advantages, and then compare them with the disadvantages. If you can live with the worse case scenario of the disadvantage, and the risk will move you towards your goal, take the risk. If you can't live with the worse possible outcome, then you should not take the risk.

> Opportunities surround us constantly. Unfortunately, many people have not been trained to recognize and identify them.

Opportunities knock at the door daily. Usually the home in which opportunity is knocking has the stereo and television's volume turned up so high, that the doorbell cannot be heard. By the time the doorbell is heard, they look through the peephole, ask who is it, unlock the deadbolt lock and open the door; the opportunity is already on the front porch of your neighbor's home.

Be swift but don't rush. If there is someone whose opinion you respect and value, take advantage of it. An ancient book of wisdom I read states that, " wisdom comes from a multitude of counselors". Keep in mind that you are solely responsible for making your own decisions. Don't be held back from success waiting on the approval of another person. We were all giving free will to choose. Choose carefully who you allow to sow word seeds into your life. If that person(s) are not in life where you want to aspire to, then you may want to consider alternative options. Many opportunities that you will be introduced to will require a solo gut instinct. Learn to rely on and trust your gut instincts.

I often teach my students to master the ability to make decisions. Right, wrong or indifferent, just make a decision. This is a critical area of learning. We typically aren't taught how to make decisions. As a child, what you eat, wear, and when to go to bed, were all decided by our parents or guardians. As you entered into the school system, your teachers then made decisions for you. As you entered into the work force, your boss began to make your decisions for you. Decisions such as how much money you will earn, what time you will become hungry, what time you will become tired and be allowed to go home to rest.

> ## Opportunities are never lost; they are just passed on to someone else ready and prepared to recognize them

Have you ever thought about the fact that what you are allowed to do or not allowed to do is based solely on the income that they pay you? The community you can afford to live in, the vehicle you drive, the schools your children are allowed to attend and the medical care they are allowed to have. Your vacation or lack of a vacation is also determined by what the boss decides for you.

At this stage in life, a person has never really been accustomed to making his or her own decisions in life. That's why it is so common to see a couple that wants to go out for dinner having such a difficult time deciding where to go. Become comfortable about deciding your own future.

My wife and I were already very successful in our Real Estate companies when we were exposed to information on developing our Business Development Firm. We always kept our options open to enhancing our current successes. There is a constant stumbling stone in so many people's road to success that is overlooked and ignored. So often people pretend that they have options! I'm 5'6" tall. I recognized early that I wasn't going to be the number one draft pick in the NBA. According to my wife, I can't sing nor dance, therefore you wouldn't catch me on the local or national music video channels. Therefore, I knew I had to focus on areas of success that would benefit my family and me. I didn't pretend that I had multi-millionaires knocking down my door to help me succeed. Besides, isn't pretending something children do?

I was looking for additional opportunities. I always loved my wife enough to step outside of any comfort zones and move forward with newfound information so that I would never become an economic girlie-man. I understood how to evaluate a business opportunity when it presented itself. We knew how to make our decisions without being subjected to the negative influences of other people. Please don't be held back in your success by allowing other people to make decisions in your life that will determine your family's financial future.

What did you do today to move toward your dream? Your dream is what disciplines you to achieve your dream. For a young athlete with aspirations of becoming a professional athlete, there will be a huge demonstration of discipline required. You must discipline yourself to achieve your own goals or you will be disciplined to achieve someone else's goal. Either way, you WILL be disciplined! Remember, you have the choice to decide.

With the Lord as my personal head, I made the decision that I will always be the protector and provider for the Harris Family. Does your family know and believe that you feel the same way about them? That requires discipline. Self discipline that is. A key to good decision-making is to make decisions and figure them out along the way. What's holding you back from who you want to be and where you want to go? The answer is YOU.

This is a sticking point for some. All success will at some point take a detour through the valley of struggle. Remember struggles are only temporary. You can't have rain without the lightening and thunder. There are three cycles every person will experience. You are either entering a storm, in the middle of a storm or just coming out of a storm. As you are exiting the storm, shake off your umbrella, hang up raincoat and store away your galoshes until the next storm. Always know that after every storm, the sun must come out and shine. Embrace the storms and learn from each one.

Success is a mindset. Either you have it or you are in the process of getting it. Books are a phenomenal source to develop and strengthen your mental muscles. From our neck down, is a minimum wage income-producing machine. From the neck up is an unlimited income-producing piece of equipment. Which do you feed the most? When was the last time you fed and fully satisfied the latter?

> The height of ignorance is thinking that you can't learn something from every person that you meet.

Books are man's best friend. (I'm not being gender specific here) Books allow for you to see the inner you. They help to make you mentally tough. Mental toughness is a prerequisite to accomplish any level of success. The puzzle is you. That puzzle can also be solved at any time. The clues to solving it can always be found in books. I'm sure you have heard the famous saying, "If you want to keep a secret, put it in a book". This statement was made because there are people who will never pick up a book pass their high school or college days.

The words that you speak will lead you to a proper mindset. Speak what you want in advance. Say your goal then move right in behind it with action. Having visual images of your goal is essential to attainment of that goal. Belief is another mandatory trait that you must possess in order to have the ability to transmit belief to those you lead in business or at home. You can learn a wealth of information by learning from and understanding people from various backgrounds. The height of ignorance is thinking that you can't learn something from every person that you meet.

Acquiring a mentor is a must in achieving success. The mentor/protégé relationship is priceless. Once you find a mentor who agrees to mentor you, value this relationship as you would a prized possession. Also it is critically important that you do your part as a protégé and be mentored. A great way to show your appreciation for your mentor is to take action on their words. Learn to invest in your financial education. Books always stay with you. There is no greater investment than the investment you place in yourself and other people. Don't put a price tag on your self-development program. Your finances are always a direct reflection of how well you educated yourself through reading books; and how often you associate with those who can share wisdom about the practical life application of what you read in books.

Listening is a skill to be honed in on to develop a great mentor/protégé relationship. Here is a listening test. Egg yolks (are) or (is) white? Neither phrase is correct because egg yolks are yellow! How did you score? It is important that everyone have his or her voices heard. The words you use towards others are important. Words can form, strengthen or even destroy relationships. Let your words feed the informational hunger of others and also quench their intellectual and spiritual thirst.

The words that you speak to yourself will reveal fear or faith. Your words feed both fear and faith. Which do you feed the most? Which ever is fed the most is the one that grows the most. To be great in any endeavor you must have rock solid faith. You must demonstrate faith that doesn't waver. People of faith are predictable. People follow people who are predictable. Live your life on purpose with purpose. Place a goal so lofty in front of you that you would be willing to trade your life for. Your level of thinking is what got you where you are today. You are exactly today in life where you choose to be.

Better keep yourself clean and bright; you are the window which you must see the world

— George Bernard Shaw

There are two ways of exerting strength: one is pushing down, the other is pulling up

— Booker T. Washington

When somebody challenges you, fight back. Be brutal, be tough.

— Donald Trump

It pays to know what you don't know.

Sean J. Harris

Chapter VI

Having a Teachable and Coachable Spirit

A PERSON WHO WON'T LISTEN CAN'T LEARN. A PERSON who won't learn and aren't willing to change is wasting your valuable time. We have all heard the saying that when the student is ready the teacher will appear. Right? This statement could not be any truer. You see, we don't know what we don't know. Successful people recognize that they don't know everything, and are smart enough to solicit the help of those who are in the know in the particular areas that they are not experts in.

Being humble is an open invitation for people to want to help you. If a sports team could win a championship all alone, would there be a need for a coaching staff? Of course not. Coaches can see what's going on in the game without physically being in the game. We all need people advising us from the sidelines with an advantageous view of the game. The coach can see things from a higher perch.

In the game of success, you will require a fully qualified coaching staff. Your coach however will expect you to be the quarterback and execute the plays of the coach's playbook. You must know the rules of the game in order to ever have the ball thrown to you. The game could never be won if the ball is never thrown to you to score points. To be coached properly you must first show up on the practice field. Does your coach even know whether or not you want to play? You have to be dressed out in practice uniform. Having the proper equipment is essential.

> Successful people recognize that they don't know everything, and are smart enough to solicit the help of those who are in the know

For all of you football players, do you remember in the locker room before conquering the field of battle, how you would slap each other's helmets and padding? This was to test whether you were syked for the game and more importantly if your equipment was ready for battle. There will be times when your mentor/coach will test you and your equipment to ensure that you are ready for battle.

You will be tested physically, mentally and emotionally. Always remember that the job of the coach/mentor is to take you to championships and win. Earn your superbowl ring in your field of expertise. Be very teachable and coachable to ensure a spot on your coach's team and not to be traded or become a free agent!

Being teachable is a spirit you must have from within. At any point that you feel that you can't be taught or learn something new, you just placed yourself on the bench or worse, the cut list. To be teachable, you have got to want to learn, change and grow. You have to want to be taught. Humility goes hand and hand with having a teachable and coachable spirit. I remember how teachable I was learning how to ride my bike for the first time without the training wheels. My dad, brother and I went on a eight mile bike ride. Dad taught me how to paddle, how to balance and even how to coast. I was the ideal student.

> To be coached properly you must first show up on the practice field.

I was highly teachable. There was only one thing dad forgot to teach me that day. I didn't realize until I was traveling down a steep hill at mach speed, that I had not gotten to the class on braking! Remember I stated earlier, we don't know what we don't know. A large bush caught my bike, and me the same way that the safety straps on an aircraft carrier catch a fighter jet. Needless to say the class on braking became an instant on-the-job training course in those folks front yard.

During my field training as a Deputy Sheriff, my training officer taught me a valuable lesson. We were traveling down a roadway in an industrial area of the county. We were engaged in a normal conversation when suddenly he pulled the patrol car off to the side of the road and began yelling, "I'm shot"! He reached down and handed the radio transmitter to me and asked, "Where are we"! I had no clue where we were at that moment. He sat silently for a few

> Humility goes hand and hand with having a teachable and coachable spirit.

minutes. He put the car in drive and began driving again. He looked over toward me and said, "I could have died tonight because you didn't know where to send rescue". Thank God he wasn't shot. He scolded me the remainder of the shift to ensure that I understood the importance of always knowing exactly where I was no matter how many distractions that I might be facing. Being teachable and coachable could be the difference between life or death.

Always create an environment that would cause your mentor/coach to be excited about wanting to work with you. The coach that has a difficult time with a player will quickly move on to other teachable players who value and respect their time. I can't comment enough how important it is to strengthen and protect the relationship between you and your coach. Your coach will often take time away from his or her family to invest it with and in you. Ensure that their time investment will yield a high return of their investment. Don't bankrupt your coach's time.

A Sweet Lesson In Humanity

Years ago, a 10-Year-Old boy approached the counter of a soda shop and climbed on to a stool. "What does an ice cream sundae cost?" he asked the waitress. "Fifty cents," she answered. The youngster reached deep in his pockets and pulled out an assortment of change, counting it carefully as the waitress grew impatient. She had "bigger" customers to wait on. "Well, how much would just plain ice cream be?" the boy asked. The waitress responded with noticeable irritation in her voice, "Thirty-five cents." Again, the boy slowly counted his money. "May I have some plain ice cream in a dish then, please?" He gave the waitress the correct amount, and she brought him the ice cream. Later, the waitress returned to clear the boy's dish and when she picked it up, she felt a lump in her throat. There on the counter the boy had left two nickels and five pennies. She realized that he had had enough money for the sundae, but sacrificed it so that he could leave her a tip. The moral: Before passing judgment, first treat others with courtesy, dignity, and respect. Adapted from a Lifetime of Success Pat Williams Fleming H. Revell

---

A shut mouth gathers no foot.

Author unknown

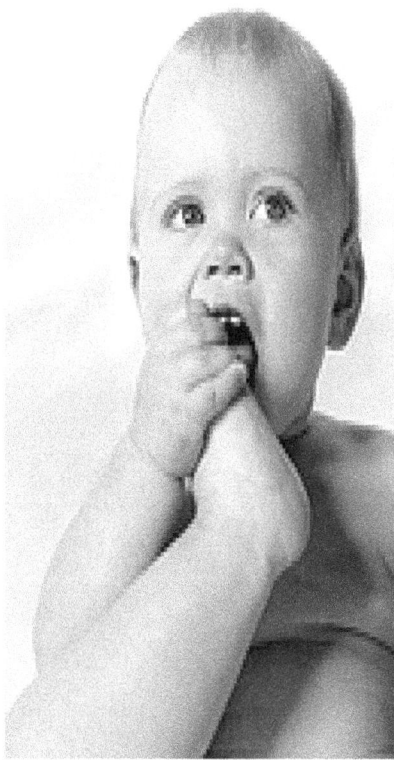

Everybody's got plans... until they get hit.

Mike Tyson

Chapter VII

Succeed When Others Fail

WINNERS WIN WHEN THOSE WHO CHOSE NOT TO WIN make excuses. You can make money or you can make excuses, but you can't make both at the same time. Excuses are the nails that are used to build the house of failure that wavers on the foundation of weakness. When your income exceeds your expenditures, you are different. There isn't room for emotions in business. It's never personal. To have your income continue growing to the next level, you must be different. You must think, perform and speak differently. Your present mindset is what got you where you are right this moment. To have better you must do better. You've got to become better by reaching your pinnacle. You must be on point and master your game.

As you encounter winners you must let winners win. That's what they do best. On the converse, you must allow losers to lose. They have their own reasons for losing, just as winners have their own reasons for winning. You must become a "Butt-kicker' in order to win. Remember, Butt-kicking begins with kicking your own butt first. Winning requires internal drive and discipline. Winning as well as all success is based on you learning from your mistakes.

> ## Excuses are the nails that are used to build the house of failure

How could you ever learn if you never make mistakes? All successes are built on failures. The proper equation isn't try-fail-quit. The proper equation is try-fail-adjust-succeed! Imagine the first time your little eight-month-old munchkin hands lost the firm grip that they once had on the coffee table. You fell and tested the cushioning of your diaper. If you never tried to walk again, could you imagine how silly you would look right now reading this book but could not walk at your age? So with that in mind, isn't it quite silly to think that you're never supposed to make mistakes?

> ## There isn't room for emotions in business

In the test kitchen of life

A young woman was complaining to her father about how difficult her life had become. He said nothing, but took her to the kitchen and set three pans of water to a boil. To the first pan, he added carrots; to the second, eggs; and to the third, ground coffee. After all three had cooked, he put their contents into separate bowls and asked his daughter to cut into the eggs and carrots and smell the coffee. "What does this all mean?" she asked impatiently.

"Each food," he said, "teaches us something about facing adversity, as represented by the boiling water." The carrot went in hard but came out soft and weak. The eggs went in fragile but came out hardened. The coffee, however, changed the water to something better.

"Which will you be like as you face life?" he asked. Will you give up, become hard- or transform adversity into triumph? As the "chef" of your own life, what will you bring to the table?

Adapted from the Access Christian Website

Don't fall before you're pushed

— English Proverb

To be a winner...fight one more round

— Unknown

I've missed more than 9000 shots in my career. I've lost almost 300 games. 26 times, I've been trusted to take the game winning shot and missed. I've failed over and over and over again in my life. And that is why I succeed.

— Michael Jordan

For everyone of us that succeeds, it's because there's somebody there to show you the way out. The light doesn't always necessarily have to be in your family; for me it was teachers and school.

— Oprah Winfrey

Chapter VIII

Thoughts On Knowing How
To Evaluate A Business

WHEN EVALUATING A BUSINESS, YOUR NEXT-DOOR neighbor or co-worker is not necessarily your best source of expertise. Think about it, if your next door neighbor or your co-worker knew anything about finances and business ownership, chances are that they wouldn't be your neighbor or working in the cubicle next to you. Now understand that if they own a successful business, disregard that last statement. However, many people would not fall into the category of business owners. Learn how to research and not just search for credible information in a business project you may be pursuing. The best suggestion would be to find someone who is successful in the exact business that you are interested in mastering.

Googling can be very resourceful, however, anyone can place any bit of information on the Internet whether it is true or not. Don't succumb to the committee of "they"! Who in the world is "they" and who authorized their credibility? If you listen to unproven people and take their advice, you deserve exactly less than what they have.

Many people reject what they are not familiar with. Because we may not be familiar or knowledgeable on a certain subject, doesn't make the information untrue. Always keep an open mind to information that you may not have had the privilege to learn about. Familiarity breeds contentment that results in mediocrity. There is a saying that the mind is like a parachute; it only works when it's open. The brain is the most unused possession that we have.

> **If your next door neighbor or your co-worker knew anything about finances and business ownership, chances are that they wouldn't be your neighbor or working in the cubicle next to you.**

Evaluate the people involved with the projects that you are researching. Use your instincts here. Have you ever noticed how a dog can sense if you are afraid of it? Of course I'm not comparing people to dogs, I'm only using an analogy here. People have a keen sense about determining the spirit of other people. This is where character and integrity comes into play. People are what teams consist of.

The product to be marketed is not the most important concern. With a strong team of upwardly mobile people, you could sell toothpicks and earn a fortune. However you could sell high-end Rolex watches with a terrible team, or group for that matter, and fail miserably. A group is two or more people with no leadership or coach. A team is a unified and organized unit of people with a common goal. Have you ever heard of a football group? Of course not, it's a football team. They all wear the same uniforms with one team name on the jersey.

An individual or a group can win a game but teams win championships and create dynasties. Look at the business and determine if the results it can produce will align with the dreams and goals that are important to you. Will the business that you are seeking allow for more time with your family? Will it provide you with a solid source of residual income?

> # The most successful, fastest growing and profitable businesses are those that are operated from the home.

Business ownership has changed over the past decade. The most successful, fastest growing and profitable businesses are those that are operated from the home. The goal of every business owner is to minimize expenses while maximizing profits. This is accomplished with home-based businesses due to low overhead. Personal franchised type businesses are the wave of the future. This type of business is typically accomplished through a multi-level marketing business. Don't be guided down a road of gloom and doom by the committee of "they". People who are not in the know will make the most unintelligent comments about multi-level marketing companies. Yes there are some bad ones out there just the same as there are bad people in your current profession. People who truly understand business and success, know that these types of businesses can be the best type of businesses where the everyday common person can own and live an extraordinary lifestyle. There are some great businesses out there that operate with this type of structure.

Again, don't let these uninformed people throw words around loosely. Words such as pyramid. Usually people who say those types of things are not economically successful. All businesses that succeed are structured with some type of hierarchy. Chances are where you work; there is a CEO, a couple of Vice-Presidents, a handful of upper management personnel, then a whole bunch of worker bees. Hmm, does this suggest that your place of employment is a pyramid? When language such as this is spoken to a successful person, immediately it is revealed that such a person making the comment isn't enjoying the fruits of success.

My purpose isn't to lead you to any particular business. A good rule of thumb is to find one that offers products and services that everyone needs, will use up and must be replenished. This will put you in a good situation that will afford you an economy-proof business. You see, if you sold buggy whips for a living, you probably wouldn't be doing too well in business unless you lived in an Amish community. A person selling ax handle wouldn't do too well today with the availability of user-friendly chainsaws. Remember the golden rule of business? Supply and demand!

> **Find one that offers products and services that everyone needs, will use up and must be replenished**

As I mentioned earlier, with the middle class shrinking in the United States and expanding globally, this is the best time to have an international business. The simplest way to do this is through business ownership via a multi-level marketing business. Your best bet would be to consider a business that is affiliated with the Internet. So many jobs are being outsourced, downsized, restructured; it all means the same thing. In the famous words of Donald Trump, "You're Fired!" Have you ever noticed that when you call a company's customer service department, you hear the automated system acknowledge for you to hold for the next available representative? Have you ever noticed how long it can take? It doesn't take that long for anyone to answer the phone and besides the company is not that busy! What you are holding for is the international connection to be completed because that representative is in a different part of the world!

A good multi-level marketing business should offer residual income that is willable for future generations. Residual income is doing something so well one time and getting paid forever for it. Multi-level marketing businesses grow exponentially through a network. In the cellular industry, you're either in the network or you're out of the network. When you're out of the network, your call is either dropped or you begin to roam. Roaming obviously is more expensive. In the near future, without a business of your own, you could be placing yourself in a roaming position. This can be costly. Evaluate wisely!

There are countless business options, multi-level marketing just happens to be one that I feel strongly about. This is my humble but accurate opinion for the masses of the people. This is an opportunity for the common everyday person to own a business that can grow internationally inexpensively. Beating the dead horse once again here, with the United States middle class shrinking and the foreign markets middle-class growing, it would be wise to further review this option. Recognize that a middle class in a growing economy will always drive that economy.

Famous professional hockey player Wayne Gretzky said that he would always skate to where the hockey puck would be, not playing it based on its current location. Learn to play the business puck where it's going. It's going to the world of multi-level marketing.

What A Personal Franchise Business Looks Like And Can Provide

This is a simple diagram of what a personal franchise type business can afford you and how it works.

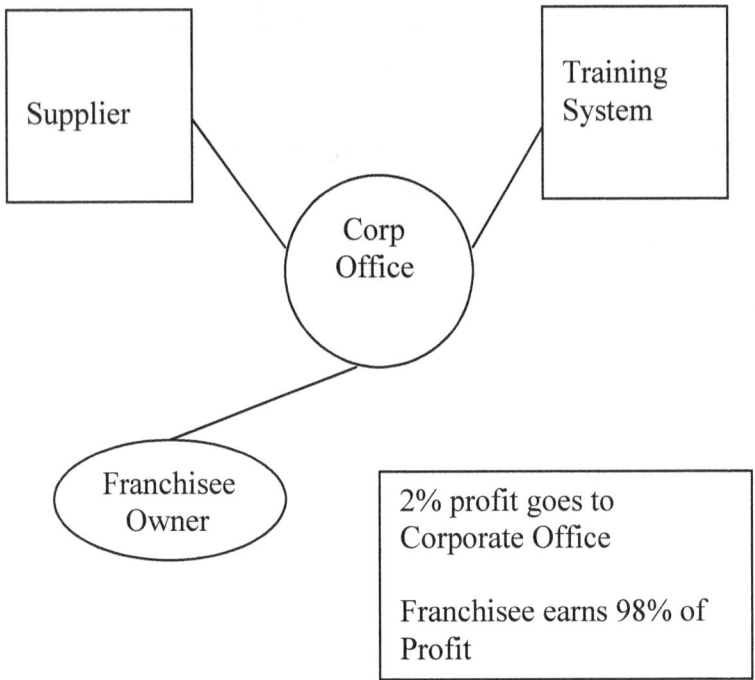

In this scenario, if the franchisee's business generated $1,000.00 per day, the franchisee would keep 98%, which is $980.00. The corporate office would earn 2% of the profit, which is $20.00. Examining this, it appears that the corporate office may not being doing as well as the franchisee. Lets assume that there were 33,000 other franchisees just like you who were paying 2% ($20.00) to the corporate office. In that case, the corporation has earned $660,000.00 in one day! Not bad huh?

The corporation helped the franchisee make a lot of money ($980.00), the corporation made a little money ($20.00), but a lot of little money (33,000) adds up to a gob of money ($660,000.00)! At this point, the franchisee duplicates and opens new outlets of business. The corporate office now pays different bonuses to incentivize the original franchisee to continue expanding. This is an absolute win-win situation.

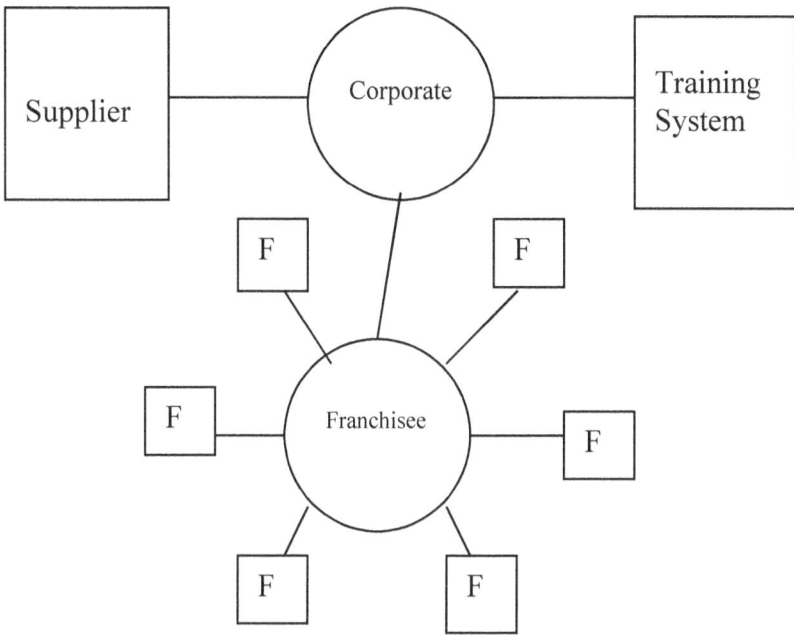

Exponential Growth takes place

A training and educational system is strongly recommended as it relates to multi-level marketing. Books, CD's, DVD's and other business support material will assist and guide you in building your own successful multi-level marketing business. Remember, your finances will always be a direct reflection on how well you have educated yourself. A personal mentor/coach is always a plus.

What you don't see with your eyes, don't invent with your mouth.

— Jewish Proverb

A wise man knows more than he tells…but a fool often tells more than he knows

— Unknown

Personality can open doors, but only character can keep them open

— Elmer G. Leterman

> "There are three things to aim at in public speaking: first, to get into your subject, then to get your subject into yourself, and lastly, to get your subject into the heart of your audience"
>
> *Alexander Gregg*

Chapter IX

The Art of Public Speaking
53 Key Guide Points

---

1. Know your subject matter

2. Speak to your audience equally

3. Brief eye contact, don't stare

4. Write names down on board if name tags are not available

5. Refer to guest by name several times

6. Use note cards if necessary

7. Don't look at the door when late comers arrive

8. Know what questions to ask

    a. What's important to you?

    b. Why is that important to you?

9. Ask questions that will warrant a positive response

10. Speak to both spouses & identify who the decision   maker is if it is a joint venture partnership

11. Know how to agree with the guest and get them to agree with you.

12. Know how to relate your business to each individual guest needs; how to bounce around and address each guest's dream when everybody's dream and goals are different

13. Educate guest in a positive non abrasive way; non confrontational

14. Move around and interact with your audience

15. Know how to set yourself at ease

16. Write large enough for audience members in the rear of the room to see

17. Repeat people's name during your discussions

18. Don't focus on one person only

19. Be excited and full of energy (Not monotone)

20. Know how to relate to the opposite sex

21. Know how and when to bring husband and wives in conversation at the right time

22. Study your audience

23. Know how to read body language

24. Don't criticize people or downplay what they do for a living

25. Know how to and when to transition the subject

    a. Don't overdo a subject or story

26. Talk about them not you

27. Don't turn your back on your audience for extended periods of time

28. Talk while you write, no dead silence

29. Re-cap your marker when not writing

30. Edify the person(s) or company that referred your guest to your event

31. Don't make guest feel like they are the only guest among colleagues, even if so

32. Don't refer to colleagues who are in attendance as if you never met them. You would need colleagues to solidify your credibility

33. Re-ignite existing colleagues

34. Use eraser not finger

35. Don't be afraid to erase

36. Learn how to be relatable

37. Know a little bit about everything (but don't be a know it all)

38. Know how to relate a situation to a person on your business team; commonalities

39. Know how to minimize and ignore distractions

40. Don't make big things out of little things

41. Don't separate spouses when talking to them, creates psychological division in their business projects before it is ever launched

42. Edify the stage you're on (The person(s) that invited you in to speak) You create credibility for that person to give strong edification

43. Don't use industry jargon that your guest will not understand

44. No team inside jokes or humor that the guest will not relate to

45. Appear confident not arrogant

46. Follow outlined steps of your agenda

47. Abbreviate when possible

48. Penmanship is not that important. (Unless it's a handwriting class)

49. Regain control after a joke

50. After your talk, receive feedback from participants

51. Ask guest what excited them the most, not what do they think (Looking for a positive response here)

52. Know what to say on stage

53. Dress appropriately

Think today and speak tomorrow

— H.C Bohn

When someone shows you who they are, believe them the first time.

— Oprah Winfrey

If you can't be a good example, then you'll just have to be a horrible warning.

Catherine Aird

Chapter X

Poor Man's Tax

HAVE YOU EVER HEARD OF THE POOR MAN'S TAX? SURE you have, it's called the lottery. You see, if your local government suggested a tax increase, chances are great that most people would object. If a politician promised you that a tax increase would be good for the community, the majority of the community would fight tooth and nail to kill the proposed tax hike.

Maybe if it were benefiting children or hospitals the community would support it. Because the government can't encourage people to support many of their tax plans, they put lotteries into place. Isn't it amazing that people would go berserk about a 2¢ sales referendum, but they will spend anywhere from

$1.00-$10.00 per day on lottery tickets! You see, the government will get their money. They will receive money in greater quantity, while the ticket buyer didn't even know what hit them.

Honestly, when was the last time you witnessed a wealthy person purchasing a lottery ticket? I just don't understand how a person who is struggling financially at times can afford to squander $10.00 a day on a pipedream. The chances of winning a windfall jackpot is as slim as getting struck by lightening twice in the same pupil at high noon on Wednesday standing next to a flagpole on a sunny day! Ten dollars per day five days per week is $50.00 per week, $200.00 per month and $2,400.00 per year. Could you imagine how many other promising places you could invest this money and receive a much better return on your investment? If you are a parent, there is a great start! Your children.

> **When was the last time you witnessed a wealthy person purchasing a lottery ticket?**

An extra $2,400.00 dollars could serve as start-up capital for your own business that could lead you to jackpot style money for the rest of your life. I have read that one out of ten businesses doesn't succeed, but those odds are a heck of a lot better than one in a gazillion! Have you noticed that lottery games have names relating to dreams and fantasies? There has never been a lottery system that has gone bankrupt. Have you ever wondered why?

Let's just suppose that a person won a lottery. Here is why most people whom win lotteries find themselves financially worse off eighteen months later. They become "New Rich". Their thought process doesn't catch up to the newfound money. Many people that I discuss this issue with always state that they would buy everything under the sun for their family and friends.

Well there is nothing wrong with having a givers heart but you must first have a givers wallet. Most would say that they would cash the check and start spending immediately. Paying off mother's house is a great idea. However, if she has ten years left on her mortgage, three more months typically would not ruin her financially if you don't pay it off immediately.

So often people lose everything because they never mastered the art of saying "No". If a person won one million dollars, it would be wise to find a way to grow that money in a relatively short period of time. Don't just blow it. Here in Atlanta, a million dollars can be easily absorbed on the purchase of a house quicker than you can say shazam!

> # There is nothing wrong with having a givers heart but you must first have a givers wallet.

Here is an intelligent suggestion. Take a portion of the winnings and invest it professionally in an area that will yield a sizeable return. Suppose we invested a portion of the winnings that yielded a $25,000.00 return from maybe an initial $5,000.00 investment. You will have only exhausted $5,000.00 to earn an additional $20,000.00. This is a total of $1,020,000.00. You have used pre-existing money to create $20,000.00, which is now used to pay off Mom's house. You have to create an income-producing asset. You will still have your initial $1,000,000.00. Please, please, please educate yourself!

You know, when writing a book, everyone wants a free copy. That's the easiest way to find yourself in the poorhouse. If you printed let's say 500 books and you allotted 50 books to be used as promotional give-aways, you would yield more sales than if you gave 50 free books to family and friends. More importantly will people who received the free book ever really read the book? Remember there is no room for emotions in business.

How well would you do in business if you were a newly established orthodontist and you gave all of your family and friends free braces? When your lease and first medical equipment bill comes due, trust me you would not be thrilled. But Sean, people would be offended. Well, offense never paid any of my bills. Again, it's not personal; it's just intelligent business.

This is where emotional stability and mental toughness enters the equation. As a leader, you lose your right to have a bad day. You must operate on an even kilt and maintain your emotions particularly when you are leading others. You no longer have the luxury of wearing your feelings on your sleeve. When people reject your ideas, you can't take it personal. Usually they are rejecting your ideas not you as a person.

What's on your mind currently? Would it be a positive event if it were broadcasted on a large movie screen for the general public to see? There is a difference between thoughts and thinking. Thoughts are random and thinking is a choice. You must know what thoughts to accept and which ones to reject. Your thoughts + action = desired results. You control your thought life through action and practice. Mental toughness is having the ability to stand and withstand no matter what the opposition is.

> **Thoughts are random and thinking is a choice**

When it comes to mental toughness, what is inside of you is greater than anything outside of you. You must learn to think on purpose. You press through difficulties by keeping your heart and mind fixed on what you want through the faith that you possess. Success is started in the mind. To succeed, you must learn to stop stopping in your endeavors. Teach yourself how to have little burst of faith. Once you grab the plow, keep your hand to the plow and keep moving forward. Motivation will then follow your actions. Remind yourself what it is that you want. Speak aloud what you are expecting. Remind yourself of the truth. And most importantly be thankful and have a grateful heart.

Truth is higher than facts. The world will fill you with facts. Facts change all the time, they are always subject to change. Don't base your destiny on facts. Base your destiny on truth. Truth is true regardless of your experience. Truth applies whether you understand it or not. If a plane went down in the mountains, the principles of aerodynamic did not stop working. They still applied. The truth didn't change only the facts.

> Mental toughness is having the ability to stand and withstand no matter what the opposition is.

If I hold a pen in the air, that becomes a fact. But when I drop the pen on the floor the facts changes. Again facts change but the truth doesn't, the truth is consistent. Live your life on the truth. There is an ancient scroll that I read written over 2000 years ago that can teach you all the truths that you will need to succeed and live a great awesome life. Don't get tired of doing the right thing. Name your dream, put a price tag on it and put a system in place that will allow for you to pay for it. At some point you must look in the mirror of truth and build your faith muscles. You have to go through difficult times to strengthen and grow your faith muscles. Mental toughness requires you to decide how you are going to do something and not focus on how you are not going to do something.

Something you get for nothing is usually worth it

— Unknown

"The lottery is a tax on people who flunked math"

— Monique Lloyd

"If you really want something in this life you have to work for it. Now quiet, they're about to announce the lottery numbers"

— Dan Castellaneta

Books were my pass to personal freedom. I learned to read at age three, and soon discovered there was a whole world to conquer that went beyond our farm in Mississippi.

Oprah Winfrey

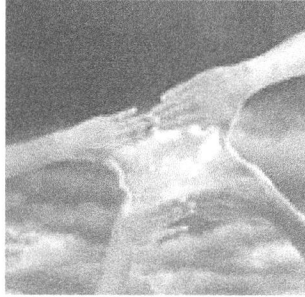

Chapter XI

---

3 Times When People Make A Change

- When they need to
- When someone shows them that change is good
- When they are prepared

As humans we are required to change naturally. As we enter into our adolescent years, we experience changes in our bodies, the way we speak and even growing taller. Change is necessary for growth. That growth can be physical growth, mental growth or emotional growth. We can't grow in any of those areas without changing what we allow to enter our minds.

We need to change when our current circumstances are no longer satisfactory. Successful people are never really satisfied. Never get comfortable in your comfort zone. All success is found outside the box. When your forward progression stops or even worse, goes backwards is definitely an indicator that you NEED to change.

With a seasoned success eye, you will recognize that change is mandatory before you begin to go backwards. You should beware when you begin to decelerate just a few miles per hours in your fast pace success vehicle. Change is a progressive activity.

Often we don't recognize that change is good. A great example; I was having a conversation with an intern that I was interviewing for consideration to joining my business development firm. I asked him if he would rather work for a company earning $125,000.00 per year or own his own business earning $100,000.00 per year? He answered with resounding "Business Ownership"! I instantly brought him aboard the firm and began to mentor him. Understand, he was willing to give up something good in exchange for something great. When someone has a valid reason for change in your life, you should honestly evaluate his or her suggestion. Many people can never see the trees for the forest. Allow for people who are proven and whose opinion you respect and value offer insight in areas you may want to consider.

> **Being prepared is instrumental for change**

After spending many years in law enforcement, I recognized that change was good. After several incidents, I really saw that an exit strategy was a good idea. I discovered very quickly in my career that I was allergic to hot lead coming in my direction! I commend all my brothers and sisters in blue out there keeping us safe.

At this point I shifted careers and launched my real estate companies which obviously were much more conducive to prolonging my good health. Starting my real estate companies afforded me more money while utilizing less time. This is a great personal example of recognizing that change was good.

After being involved in real estate for several years, I began to increase my workload by choice. Unfortunately I began losing my time again. I realized that this way of creating income was based solely on my physical ability to perform. If I ever stopped working, the income would stop coming in. This income wasn't residual either. I knew that it was time for more change. This is when I made the decision to change again. This is when I launched my business development firm.

> ## Success is obtained only when preparedness and opportunity co-exist.

Being prepared is instrumental for change. A friend may suggest that you need to change your diet and workout regime. You even accept the fact that changing your diet and workout regime would be a good change. However, if you are not prepared to purchase a gym membership and go to the gym consistently, it's all in vain.

We have all heard the saying that success is obtained only when preparedness and opportunity co-exist. Are you currently prepared for change in your life? Are you prepared to learn new information that is vital to your success? Too often people look for excuses to stay exactly where they are now.

Wisdom is divided into two parts: (1) having a great deal to say, and (2) not saying it

— Unknown

A sharp tongue and a dull mind are usually found in the same head

— Unknown

Education is when you read the small print. Experience is what you get if you don't .

Pete Seeger

Chapter XII

Understanding The Difference
Between W-2 and 1099 Income

The information contained herein should not be used in any actual transaction without the advice and guidance of a professional Tax Advisor who is familiar with all the relevant facts. The information contained here is General in nature and is not intended as legal, tax or investment advice. Furthermore, the information contained herein may not be applicable to or suitable for the individuals' specific circumstances or needs and may require consideration of other matters. Neither the author nor the publishing company assumes any obligation to inform any

person of any changes in the tax law or other factors that could affect the information contained herein.

W-2 income is merely based on trading time for money working a job. W-2 basically means (W) withholding (2) too much money! Usually a person in this category files a 1040EZ tax return. If your taxes are EZ to file, usually you are easily loosing too much money. So often I see people get so excited to receive a tax refund.

> # If you live in a country that allows you the freedom to own your own business, why wouldn't you?

They jump for joy saying, " I'm getting $2500.00 this year". Well what's really taking place her is very simple. You are receiving your own money back on the loan that the government borrowed forcefully for the past year, and they kept the interest. It was your money in the first place. Who got the better end of that stick? Doesn't seem fair huh? Well you can do something about it. You can start your own business. Understand that the tax laws were written for business owners not employees. If you live in a country that allows you the freedom to own your own business, why wouldn't you? Life is asking you a question. Wouldn't you like to give yourself a raise rather than to beg for one? With W-2 income, you are taxed on the front end. Your gross income is taxed which could make your net income seem really gross to look at.

Picture this; you get a paycheck that has already been taxed. You purchase eggs, milk and butter which has tax attached to them. You are paying taxes on items with after-taxed dollars. How could you ever get ahead? This is a sure way to remain behind the eight ball in your finances.

1099 Income is quite different and provides you with a breath of fresh air. The self-employed, investors and business owners enjoy this type of income. The business owner can enjoy the fruits of his or her labor, while paying their taxes after their money is created. Suppose that an employee earned $100k this year and a business owner also earned $100k this year. The employee is taxed upfront. The business owner may have $75k in expenses and other tax deductions. This leaves the business owner $25k that is taxable. Both the employed person and the business owner earned $100k this year, however we must recognize who kept the most. In this case of course it was the business owner.

Employee   Business Owner

As an employee, to create more money, you would have typically had to work more hours or pick up a second job. Have you ever noticed that if a person got a second job part time, they are usually paid less money than what they earn on their primary job. If a third job were required, it would pay them even less than the second job. Keep in mind here that your time commitment continues to increase.

With W-2 income your finances will resemble the illustration below. With 1099 income, having a business system in place will enable you to leave a legacy for future generations.

Growth differences between W-2 and 1099 Income

Three Generations with W-2 income.

Multiple Generations with System driven 1099 income

In the diagrams above, the first illustration depicts three generations with each generation only accomplishing what the previous generation had accomplished relying solely on W-2 income. The younger generations can't pick up where the previous generation had left off in their profession. A child can't go to his parent's place of employment after twenty years and ask the employer to join the company at the same level in which their parents had retired. However, in the second illustration, a parent can leave an established business for their children to continue at the same level of success. This type of business can be left as a legacy for several generations. This is why I favor businesses structured as a multi-level marketing business. Choose a good one however. Look for one that provides a product or service that everyone can benefit from and afford. Choose a multi-level business in which the product or service will be used up and must be replenished frequently. This is how longevity and stability is created.

Michael Jordan, Tiger Woods, and Elvis Presley are all great examples of how income is passed from generation to generation. If you don't have athletic, singing or acting abilities, you may want to strongly consider thoroughly researching a multi-level marketing business. It's the best opportunity for the everyday common person to live an extraordinary lifestyle.

> If you don't have athletic, singing or acting abilities, you may want to strongly consider thoroughly researching a multi-level marketing business.

Part of being a winner is knowing when enough is enough. Sometimes you have to give up the fight and walk away, and move on to something that's more productive.

— Donald Trump

Sometimes by losing a battle you find a new way to win the war.

— Donald Trump

I'm not out there sweating for three hours every day just to find out what it feels like to sweat.

Michael Jordan

My body could stand the crutches but my mind couldn't stand the sideline.

Michael Jordan

Chapter XIII

Playing Hurt

ALL WINNERS AT SOME POINT WILL PLAY HURT DURING their journey to the end zone, across the finish line or across home plate. I recall watching footage and photos of the players on the Green Bay Packer's football team during the Vince Lombardi era. These battle-tested, battered and bruised giants played in the worse environments and conditions. Could you imagine busting your knuckles in ten below zero weather? Imagine playing with broken noses, broken fingers and cracked rib cages in Antarctic conditions. These guys did! These giant warriors experienced burning lungs from the dense frozen air traveling through their mucus filled nasal cavities. There was no such thing of having the luxury of a climate-controlled dome to conduct brutal battle on the Gridiron. This was hardcore football!

Could you imagine a player going up to Lombardi and whine, "It's a little chilly out here coach". Or coach, "I think I hurt my pinky finger. Can I go sit on the bench?" I just couldn't ever imagine any of those players doing that. Becoming a champion will hurt.

I remember watching the 2007 Wimbledon Tennis Championship on television. Champion tennis player Serena Williams was battling to advance to the quarterfinals. Suddenly, Serena crashed to the grass surface during her second set with a severe cramp in her left calf. You could see the calf muscle flinch, as a sizeable knot began to form.

Becoming a champion will hurt.

Serena's training staff rushed to her side as she lay on the court in excruciating pain. As she clutched her calf, she was treated on the court by the medical staff. She could hardly move, however she managed to get back on her feet hobbling around on one leg. A two-hour rain delay enabled her to get more extensive treatment and returned to compete. She managed to achieve a three set victory, though she was in great pain and discomfort.

Serena later said that she thought about not finishing, but only for a brief moment. She said that she didn't think she would be able to live with herself if she had not at least tried. See, that's the language of a champion! Having so much passion for what you love, that you couldn't possibly live with yourself if you quit. Champions aren't designed to quit. As a matter of fact, they don't even know how to spell the word!

Serena's will to win was undoubtedly stronger than any pain that she experienced in her cramp stricken calf. I remember how she whacked her calf muscle three times with her tennis racket along the baseline. When she returned to complete the set, she had both calves heavily wrapped and taped. She also had on long white pants beneath her skirt to protect her leg muscles from the cool temperatures.

Serena said that she was so motivated to win and that she would be willing to die trying. Nothing of significance can be achieved with a crybaby attitude. Are you willing to whack whatever is cramping your style to succeed? Will you get back up one more time, with blood gushing from your nose and mouth? Will you be willing to keep playing and find your missing tooth later? Are you willing to bandage up heavily and keep going? Are you the type that says, "Coach, put me back in the game?" There's no glory on the bench!

I wrestled in high school. My senior year was a memorable year for me. I recall competing in a tournament in which the top athletes in the southeastern region of the United States qualified to compete. There were college and Olympic scouts in the arena. I had made it to the finals. It was a tough journey filled with injuries. There we were, in a deafening arena with the fans cheering, camera's flashing, and the smoke machine infusing smoke into the entrance tunnel. The spot light was set on my adversary and I. At the time, I was in so much pain from compounded injuries over the season that had come to a head that tournament. Warriors will play hurt the whole season just to make it to this crowning moment. My right knee had been hyper-extended several times that season. My thumb was fractured and heavily taped. I found out several years later through an x-ray that it had been fractured. My rib cage was bruised.

Champions aren't designed to quit

The top two wrestlers in the southeastern United States stood there facing one another. One would go home the victor and the other in defeat. Years of hard work and dedication would reflect. He stood in my way to victory and I in his, to becoming the number one athlete in the southeastern region of this country.

My will not to lose was far greater than the pain emanating throughout my body. I wanted to win more than my opponent's will not to lose. I just kept reflecting back to all the hard days and endless nights of grueling practices and preparations for this one moment in time. I reached deep down and pulled the inner champion out to partner with the outer champion. The athlete with the strongest desire to triumph and win will always come out the victor. I have never let an opponent's desire out shine mine. I was the victor who pushed the envelop through the hurt and pain, and became a champion that day.

> # There's no glory on the bench!

Some learn from experience others never recover from it

— **Unknown**

When you win nothing hurts

— **Joe Namath**

Bad is never good until worse happens

— **Danish Proverb**

Do the one thing you think you cannot do. Fail at it. Try again. Do better the second time. The only people who never tumble are those who never mount the high wire. This is your moment. Own it.

— **Oprah Winfrey**

All the adversity I've had in my life, all my troubles and obstacles, have strengthened me... You may not realize it when it happens, but a kick in the teeth may be the best thing in the world for you.

— **Walt Disney**

If money titles meant anything, I'd play more tournaments. The only thing that means a lot to me is winning. If I have more wins than anybody else and win more majors than anybody else in the same year, then it's been a good year.

Tiger Woods

Chapter XIV

Never Hold A Winner
Back from Winning

WINNERS ARE DESIGNED TO WIN, SO DON'T HINDER THEIR victory. You should never feel intimidated by a winner on your team. In a football huddle, the players already know the play. The huddle is there for unity and encouragement. The coaches allow the quarterbacks the opportunity to go out there and win games. The coach many times let the quarterback run with his ideas.

Room must be left for winners to make decisions. They should be allowed to learn and grow from the decisions that they made on their own. When a winner isn't allowed to win, they will either become less creative or move to a team where they can excel and win. Most will choose the latter option. A winner who is stifled will feel as though he or she is like a bridled stallion in a barn full of mules. Stallions are bred to run and not be a show horse on a carousel or in a parade of mediocrity.

As a kid, my Dad, brother and I ran road races. When I was seven years old, we ran a three-mile race. We always trained hard for each race. This particular race, I just couldn't make it past the two and a half mile marker. We were always taught that no warrior would ever be left on the battlefield. My Dad stopped and placed me on his shoulder and said let's finish the race. Success is built on the shoulders of giants. My dad has always been my hero.

> # When a winner isn't allowed to win, they will either become less creative or move to a team where they can excel and win.

Ten years later, my dad and I ran the world famous Peachtree Road Race in Atlanta, Georgia. This is a six-mile event. Runners from all around the globe travel to Atlanta to run this race. At this point in my life I was very athletic and conditioned. I had been training vigorously to prepare for basic training to enter the United States Air Force. My dad and I were running side by side for the first three miles. My plans were to run the race together with dad. He looked over at me the way a lion would look at its cub to release him into the wild. Dad said, "son go run your race, I'll see you at the finish line." There was a passing team of Army guys running that I joined. I jumped right into formation with them and followed their cadence for the remainder of the race. Dad knew that I could run harder and that he didn't want to hold me back in the race or in life. This was a valuable lesson on life for me. It was a subtle teaching point that my dad had a great talent of doing. Know when to release the cub in your life into the jungle of life to survive on his or her own. Trust that the values and lessons that you instilled will carry them through the difficulties and on to victories. This is true for your children as well as people you lead professionally. I was at the finish line with a cup of Gatorade waiting for dad. You see, you never take for granted those who helped you arrive to the point you're at in life.

A child's life is like a piece of paper on which every person leaves a mark

— Chinese proverb

The average human heart beats 100,000 times a day. Make those beats count

— Unknown

Character is made by what you stand for; reputation by what you fall for

— Robert Quillen

Lots of people want to ride with you in the limo, but what you want is someone who will take the bus with you when the limo breaks down.

Oprah Winfrey

I still have my feet on the ground, I just wear better shoes.

Oprah Winfrey

Chapter XV

Dream Circle vs. Income Circle

As we aged from childhood to adulthood, we had visions of where we would be in life at various ages. We thought that when we turned sixteen years old that we would have the nicest car of all of our friends. How many of us would have been happy just to get a car at sixteen? When we turned eighteen we were going to…, when we turned twenty-one, twenty-five and thirty, we were going to…, whatever it may have been. We probably reached all of those ages and didn't quite accomplish what we set out for.

Well we're supposed to have dreams and visions. The Bible teaches us that a man or woman without vision shall perish. We all formed a dream circle in our youth. These circles may have consisted of our dream homes, cars, where we would like to travel. The cool things we would like to do for and with our parents and loved ones.

We dreamed about solving our financial deficits. Being able to have a "peace" of mind. How awesome would it be to finally pay off the student loan people? Have you ever noticed how they can locate you wherever you may go? I always said that if the government really wanted to find Osama, send the student loan folks out to find him! Many people have visions of giving to charity. I wanted to give to charities whereby I wasn't the recipient of that charity.

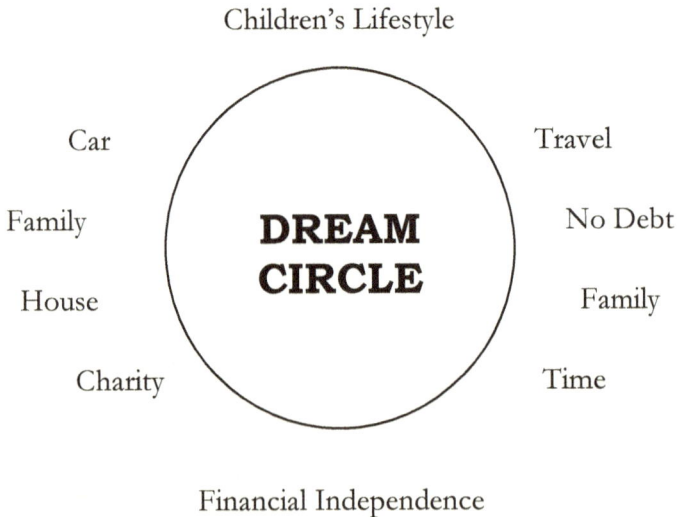

Children's Lifestyle

Car

Family

House

Charity

DREAM CIRCLE

Travel

No Debt

Family

Time

Financial Independence

Unfortunately as we begin to work, our income circle is so small that we can place numerous income circles within the confines of the dream circle with plenty of room to spare. So often we begin to live a settle-for lifestyle. We begin to shrink our dream circle to meet our income circle. We settle for a car that will get us from point "A" to point "B", regardless of its safety. Would you feel at ease in a nice luxury sedan or SUV with a gazillion airbags? You would probably feel like an over protected egg, but you would be very safe.

I have seen some cars that would topple over if a mosquito hit the windshield. How safe could this possibly be? Isn't it a greater benefit to you and your family to be in a vehicle with GPS tracking features? Medical and rescue could be enroute to you even if you are incapacitated. Could you imagine how dreadful it could be in the ditch sideways in an unsafe car with no cell phone service?

> A man or woman
> without vision
> shall perish.

I hear so many people make the following statement. As a matter of fact, you will be able to complete this sentence. Ready? "Why would a person want to live in a house that large? Who's going to … go ahead you complete this sentence. You got it. They ask, "Who's going to clean it?" News flash. If you can afford to live in such a home, trust me, you will be able to afford to hire someone to clean it.

I'm not intending for you to be materialistic here. Having nicer or even more expensive things could be the difference that could save your life one day. The lack of money can kill you one day. I've been to countless automotive establishments where an adult can't simply purchase a set of four brand new tires at one time. I've seen people negotiate which tire can get by until the next pay period. They argue that they can ride on that tire for another three months even though the radials are exposed and causing sparks to fly from the roadway!

Money isn't everything, but it sure is as important as oxygen. Without it, life sucks. It's a good idea to increase your income circle to meet and surpass your dream circle, rather than to shrink your dream circle to match your income circle.

> Money isn't everything, but it sure is as important as oxygen

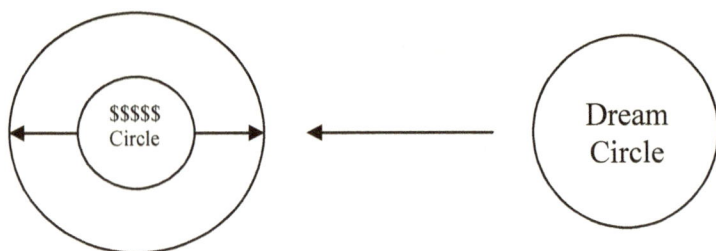

Increase Income Circle

How do I increase my income circle you may be asking? Well, my preference is through developing a business of your own. A system driven business is the best in my humble opinion. When we need more money, we typically work more hours or acquire a secondary job. Both of these options require time. Usually time we really didn't have to spare in the beginning. Did you know that with only a fraction of the time that you spend, (not invest) in a second part-time job is all you need to start your own business? Or you may have been taught to go back to school and receive more education. Ok, picture this. You completed you bachelor's degree and have a balance of $30k of student loans. You luckily received a job in the same field as your degree. This is becoming a rarity you know. You are now earning $40k a year. You hit the proverbial glass ceiling and are told that you need another degree with more education. You go back to school requiring more student loans of $25k because you have yet to satisfy your initial loan. Now you received a higher education with $55k in student loans. You expect to get the enormous raise now.

You recognize that you only made an extra $7.50 per pay period after taxes were accounted for. You ask yourself, "What was all that about?" It becomes a perpetual cycle of unending torment to you and your purse. You would fare much better taking a small percentage of that loan and starting your own business. There are countless business options that you can start on a shoestring budget. Henry Ford started the Ford Corporation on his kitchen table! Michael Dell launched Dell Computer from his college dorm room. What can you start with what you currently have? Go for it! You can do it! Fulfill your dream with your own dream and not the limited dreams that a job thrust upon you based on your income. Become the architect of your own dream circle.

> ## Become the architect of your own dream circle.

As long as you're going to be thinking anyway, think big.

— Donald Trump

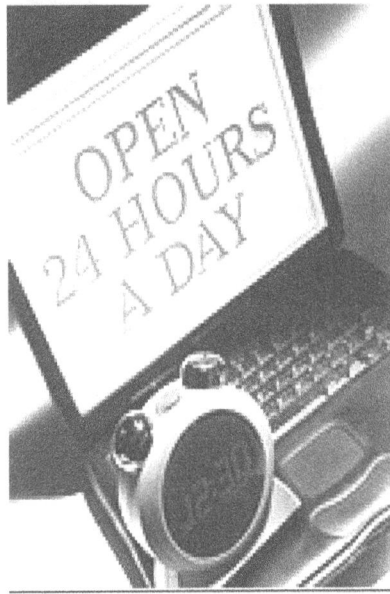

OPEN
24 HOURS
A DAY

**The mind is like a
parachute, it only
works when it's open.**

Author Unknown

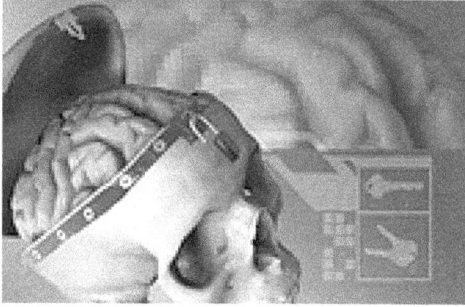

Chapter XVI

Protecting Your Mental PC

WITH ALL OF THE ADVANCES IN TECHNOLOGY, THERE IS so much that can be done through the use of computers. Do you guys remember the first computers that were offered to the public? It was nearly the size of a coffee table. You would reach in the very rear of the unit to turn it on. Do you remember when a floppy disk was really floppy?

We were told never to touch the little window where the disk was exposed. I want to let you in on a little secret. Shhhh. I touched it ALL THE TIME! Nothing ever happened. These computers had the huge block cursor with an analog screen. You would have to type in all sorts of letters and characters to use it. Just look at the quantum leap that has been made in the world of computers. Computers can really do some amazing things today.

I don't believe that there is a human on earth today that doesn't have some sort of anti-virus protection software installed. As great as the computer is today, a greater computer created it, which is the human brain. What type of anti-virus have you uploaded for protection on your mental PC?

Follow me through a scenario please. Imagine your neighbor coming over to your home. You have beautiful bright white plush carpet in your family room. Very expensive carpet might I add. Your neighbor enters with a wheelbarrow filled with foul smelling trash and left over food. The odor

> **Have you invested in an anti-virus for your mind?**

would even run skunks and vultures away. The wheelbarrow was dripping with a weird colored fluid caused from fermentation. Your neighbor dumped the contents in the center of the floor and smeared the waste around, deeply embedding it into the carpet fibers. The neighbor turns to leave your home. What would you do?

You would probably go ballistic. You would ask why did they do such a thing. You would insist that they replaced your carpet. You may even get to the point of physical altercation. Isn't it thought provoking how we can go overboard to protect our physical property and not allow people to damage or destroy it? We would be so consumed with our property.

Well if we wouldn't let someone dump trash in our physical living rooms, why on earth do so many people allow people to dump trash in the living room floor of their minds? And won't even question it the way we would the trash on our carpet. Have you invested in an anti-virus for your mind? Your anti-virus for your mental PC consist of books, positive mental attitude audio materials and positive associations. Just as your desktop anti-virus can expire, so can your mental PC's anti-virus. You must keep your screen refreshed.

It requires frequent uploads and updates to ensure maximum security to prevent any viruses. Don't allow your mental PC to receive spam and pop-ups. By protecting your hard drive, you protect your future. A good mentor or coach serves as your software consultant and technician. This will protect you from the vicious hackers who live to destroy your hard drive.

> # By protecting your hard drive, you protect your future

Success or failure in business is caused more by mental attitude even than by mental capacities

— Walter D. Scott

Our ideas, like orange plants, spread out in proportion to the size of the box, which imprisons the roots

— Edward George Bulwer-Lytton

You pray for rain, you gotta deal with the mud too. That's a part of it.

Denzel Washington

Chapter XVII

Peaks And Valleys

ON A VOYAGE OR JOURNEY TOWARDS SUCCESS, YOU WILL encounter both peaks and valleys. Psalms 23:4, yea though I walk through the valley of the shadow of death, I will fear no evil: for thou art with me; thy rod and thy staff they comfort me. This scripture states the shadow of death, not death itself.

The shadow of an object can't harm you. Always remember that a shadow cannot be casted without light coming from somewhere. Light is life. There will always be light as you trudge through the valley. You will learn and grow when you are in the valley. This time of education and wisdom development is required for growth.

When you are at the peak, you should demonstrate a humble and grateful heart. At this point you have been tested to be able to share your testimony, and aid someone else in his or her journey. The valleys are where you will toughen and develop character-building qualities. This is where you will develop strength by exercising and flexing your faith muscles.

> ### Valleys are where you will toughen and develop character-building qualities.

Most of the successful individuals that I know attribute their success to their spiritual faith. Where you are in life is spiritual. No matter what your faith is, I believe that you must rely on a greater being. Because everything is created by something greater than they are. A house cannot create a person, however a person can create a house. How can a person value him or herself and have a high self-image of them if they believe that they came from a monkey. Food for thought here. If humans evolved from monkeys, why are there still monkeys in existence today?

If you left one thousand dogs on a deserted island and came back a thousand years later, what will you find? **_DOGS!!!_** Not humans. Whatever your spiritual beliefs are, gain wisdom. If you feel that you are troubled on your road to success, study and reflect back on your spiritual walk. Don't fall into the river of complacency; otherwise you will drift into a sea of uncertainty and be dumped into an ocean of mediocrity.

Worry is a misuse of the imagination

— Dan Zadra

If you're going through hell, keep going.

— Winston Churchill

If you break your neck, if you have nothing to eat, if your house is on fire, then you got a problem. Everything else is inconvenience.

— Robert Fulghum

We have no right to ask when sorrow comes, "Why did this happen to me?" unless we ask the same question for every moment of happiness that comes our way.

— Author Unknown

There are two ways of spreading light: to be the candle or the mirror that reflects it

Edith Wharton

Chapter XVIII

Crystallizing Your Vision

IF A PERSON IS PASSIONATE ABOUT A VISION, IT SHOULD BE easily recognizable. If someone entered your home, there should be clear-cut signs of what is important to you. You should have obvious signs and reflections of your goals and visions.

For a teenager who has dreams of becoming a collegiate or professional athlete, he or she will most likely have posters displayed all over their bedroom walls. They will likely have photos of their favorite athlete. Maybe they will even have a photo of that athlete with them in the photo as well. You may find a ticket stub from a previous game that they attended. Perhaps you may find an autographed ball on the bookshelf.

Understand that if a person has great aspirations of moving on to a professional level, their vision must be clearly defined and posted everywhere for them to consistently see it daily. Remember, out of sight out of mind.

I bought my first plastic barbell weight set when I was nine years old. I remember saving up my allowance until I had accumulated $19.00. It was a twenty-pound barbell set with four maroon 4.4 lbs plates with a hollow metal bar. Life couldn't be any better! Every boy in the neighborhood had a desire to have one. I was geared and ready to begin my road to becoming MR. Universe!

As I began a consistent routine, my parents recognized that I was serious about weight training. For my following birthday, mom and dad bought a weight bench for me. I didn't have much room in my bedroom for my newly expanded home gym, however my parents allowed me to set up shop in the garage.

I began to acquire more weights a few plates at a time. I started to make great physical gains. In order to remain focused, I began to purchase bodybuilding books and magazines. I cut out pictures of all of my favorite bodybuilders and plastered all of the walls in the garage with my heroes in bodybuilding. There were no bare spots left on the walls.

> To help you crystallize your vision is to place photos on your refrigerator, bathroom mirror, your dashboard or any other place that will cause you to see it several times daily

I picked out the photos of the guys with the types of chest, arms, legs and back that I wanted to develop. This provided a roadmap for what I wanted to achieve. I remember how cold it would become in the wintertime in the garage. My mom would peep in and ask if I were ok. She would see my focus and intensity and just smile and shake her head. I could see in her eyes that she was proud to have given birth to such a winner. She gave birth to three great winners. My mother instilled so many countless values and life lessons in me. My mom has always demonstrated the qualities of a proverbs 31 woman.

The hours that I spent in that garage, looking at those photos on a daily basis, inspired me. They guided and encouraged me on my road to becoming a competitive bodybuilder. That experience led me to be selected as a member on the U.S. Air Force Bodybuilding Team.

A good idea to help you crystallize your vision is to place photos on your refrigerator, bathroom mirror, your dashboard or any other place that will cause you to see it several times daily. If I came to your home, would there be sufficient evidence to convict you of being guilty of chasing your dream?

If you have a goal of buying an expensive sports car, you should attain a brochure from the dealership. Place a photo of it somewhere that will cause you to be reminded of it continuously. Upload the image on your screensaver. If homes are your thing, go visit the type of home that you would like to own. Take photos of the most exciting parts of the home. I would suggest contacting a realtor and inform them that you plan to be in a position to purchase that particular home in a designated time frame. I would recommend attending open house events and home shows.

You must right your vision down on paper for it to have power. In the Bible, Habakkuk 2:2 teaches us to write the vision and make it plain on tablets, that he may run who reads it. Great things happen when you write them down. This is a principle that can advance your financial future to change your options and change your control factor.

You'll find things to be just the way you think they are

— Positive Christian website

So go ahead. Fall down. The world looks different from the ground.

— Oprah Winfrey

You can have it all. You just can't have it all at once.

— Oprah Winfrey

If you think big, small problems won't matter.

Sean J. Harris

Chapter XIX

Leaning Forward Towards Success

LITTLE THINGS MAKE THE BIGGEST DIFFERENCES IN LIFE. Have you ever watched a football game where it was obvious that a receiver was about to score a touchdown? After all of their showboating towards the end zone, from out of nowhere comes a cornerback with lightening speed to prevent him from scoring a winning touchdown. What caused him to be caught?

Here is another scenario. The same receiver is wide open to receive a pass, when in his peripheral vision; he witnesses and hears the footsteps from a determined cornerback coming right towards him. Moments later, he didn't catch the ball. Both instances were the result of broken focus. Focus is essential when it comes to succeeding.

The receiver in the first scenario didn't hear the footsteps of the fast approaching cornerback. The second scenario, the footsteps were heard. When the cornerback is in hot pursuit of the receiver, he begins to run on the tip of his toes for optimal speed, the same way in which an Olympic runner would. The receiver couldn't hear the runner coming, which was the cause of his failure to score. In any case, the little things made the big difference.

> ## Focus is essential when it comes to succeeding.

You can't go where you don't know that you want to go. That receiver thought that he wanted to go to the end zone, however he was not 100% focused. He was not leaning forward towards successfully crossing into the end zone. He was leaning backwards.

The slight difference of one degree is all the difference between an egg boiling or a steam ship to move forward. At 211°, water is just hot. One more degree and it begin to boil. So many people are so close to operating at 212° but fall short one degree. Strive daily to operate your life at 212°. That one-degree will set you apart from the masses. This is the area in which champions live and operate. At 212° your self-image is strengthened. You can see the landscape with a clearer view. This will enable you to make better quality decisions in your entire quest. Every person is engineered for success. No one really wants to operate at lukewarm temperatures. The sea of mediocrity is lukewarm.

We all have seeds of greatness within us. These seeds allow us to overcome struggles. We are equipped to have big dreams. Along with big dreams come big struggles, which rewards us with big prizes. Little dreams carry little struggles, which yields little victories.

Do you want small blessings for your family or large blessings? Small plans take just as much energy as do big plans, so why waste energy on the small things? We must develop a trained mindset to dream and think on a larger scale. Speaking positive

> **You can't go where you don't know that you want to go.**

affirmations over our lives and the lives of others are instrumental in developing a trained mind. Maintaining an untrained mind will result in a life of unfulfilled wishes.

To lean forward towards success, requires a fearless attitude. A person can only travel so high harboring fear in their life. God did not put a spirit of fear in us. Fear is acquired. I will buy the fact that a person has fear for about two days, after that it's an excuse!

Having a Positive Mental Attitude is a shared trait among successful individuals. Before something is materialized, it must first become a seed of thought. Our thoughts are then transferred into our speaking. Once we apply action to our thoughts, our desired results are manifested. Once the conscious mind relays the

> **No one really wants to operate at lukewarm temperatures.**

information to the subconscious mind, the thought or idea begins to take root. A positive mental attitude generates more energy than a negative mental attitude. Be mindful that a negative mental attitude has enough energy to begin diluting the positive energies.

It's the rotten apple in a barrel analogy. One hundred good apples can never turn a rotten apple into a good one. However, the rotten apple can indeed destroy the entire barrel of apples. This is why it is imperative that the negative thoughts be removed from our thinking. We live at the level in which we think and speak. We must speak life and never death as we communicate daily with ourselves first, as well as others.

Cleansing our mental PC will enable us to always be in a learning and receptive mode towards achieving our success. Set your mind and keep it set. You have to control your mind. What is in your mind will eventually come out of your mouth.

Having a positive mental attitude will detour you from the trap of complacency. The price to pay for success is to let go of complacency. You can develop a positive mental attitude by reading self-help books and listening to empowering positive audio material. Associations with positive uplifting people will aid in your road to success. On that road to success, always

> **With big dreams come big struggles, which rewards us with big prizes**

be on the lookout for road signs. Clues to success are found all over the place. Have you ever walked pass a penny on the sidewalk without picking it up? That's how success clues are. They are everywhere, you must understand the value of them and make the choice to bend over and pick them up. Don't neglect them the same way you may a penny!

As we practice positive mental attitude principles, we will understand and better apply them in our lives. Because negative influences surround us constantly, we must be inoculated regularly with positive thoughts to reinforce our positive mental attitude. We control what our minds accept and rejects. Our mind is like any other muscle in our body and must be conditioned and developed to strengthen.

Without a constant infusion of a positive mental attitude, our mind will experience mental atrophy and decay. When a definite of purpose exist, a burning passion and desire from within will help you to focus your energy into goal attainment. When leaning forward towards success, you must be willing to go the extra mile and travel beyond the areas in which others won't go. When you do more than what is expected, your rewards will be more than expected in the long run.

On every journey to success, opposition and defeat will be encountered. Rarely is defeat permanent. From out of weakness comes strength. To succeed, an attitude of "win or perish" must be adopted. You will always win when you make up

> **To lean forward towards success, requires a fearless attitude**

in your mind to do so. We must experience an unlearning process to eliminate negative thoughts. Negative thought habits must be deliberately unlearned and cleansed from our mental hard drive. Replacing bad habits with good habits are a part of maintaining a positive mental attitude.

It is unusual to see anyone enjoy success and victory without some form of enthusiasm. Enthusiasm has been described as "God Within". Enthusiasm is a mainstay for reaching any worthwhile goal. Think about how much you enjoy being around a person with an enthusiastic personality. They become magnetic. Having an enjoyable and pleasing personality will aid you in your pursuits of success. Enthusiasm has been compared to a person, as gasoline is to an engine of a car. It is the fuel to inspire people that you influence.

Every person will be swimming upstream most of their life.

> **I will buy the fact that a person has fear for about two days, after that it's an excuse!**

The fish that moves with the current is more than likely dead and floating! Don't be afraid to jump out front. Good leaders lead from the front. The most effective leaders are also great followers of other great leaders.

As a leader, your success will begin in the mind and eventually move to your heart. When it shifts to your heart, you are a more complete leader. John C. Maxwell defines leadership as influence. In the military and in law enforcement I had leadership by authority and intimidation, which isn't really leadership at all. The people that I had authority over were obligated to follow and were not positively influenced to follow. When you have a volunteer army following you, that's true leadership. Never give up! Don't succumb to, "It just got too hard". Fight forward and chase your dream. Remember, "I can do ALL things through Christ which strengthens me" Phil 4:13.

Only those who see the invisible can do the impossible

— Unknown

This is judgment day, I expect you to use plenty of it

— Unknown

Nothing is easy to the unwilling

— Nikki Giovanni

Freedom is never voluntarily given by the oppressor; it must be demanded by the oppressed.

— Martin Luther King, Jr.

To be successful you have to be selfish, or else you never achieve. And once you get to your highest level, then you have to be unselfish. Stay reachable. Stay in touch. Don't isolate.

— Michael Jordan

The two most important requirements for major success are: first, being in the right place at the right time, and second, doing something about it.

— Ray Kroc

I wasn't satisfied just to earn a good living. I was looking to make a statement.

— Donald Trump

Appendix A

People Of Influence In My Life

Jesus Christ
Martin Luther King Jr.
Michael Jordan
Denzel Washington
My Business Coaches
Dave Thomas
Morten Anderson
Cynthia Harris
Samuel H. Harris Jr.
Oprah Winfrey
Condoleezza Rice

Lee Haney
Donald Trump
Ray Kroc
Walt Disney
Ronnie Coleman
Serena Williams
Mike Tyson
Sam Walton
Tiger Woods
Warrick Dunn
Venus Williams

Appendix B

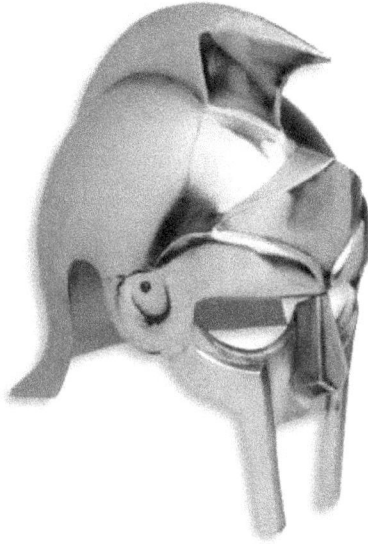

Movies That Inspired Me

Gladiator	300
Friday Night Lights	Glory Road
Remember The Titans	Braveheart
Facing The Giants	Rocky
Passion Of The Christ	Troy

Appendix C

Recommended Reading

The Holy Bible
— King James Version

The Magic of Thinking Big
— Dr. David J. Swartz

Rich Dad Poor Dad
— Robert Kiyosaki

The Millionaire Next Door
— Stanley Danko

Why We Want You To Be Rich
— Donald Trump and Robert Kiyosaki

The Business School
— Robert Kiyosaki

The Art Of The Deal
— Donald Trump

How To Develop The Leader Within You
— John C. Maxwell

The Winning Attitude
— Denis Waitley

The Power Of Focus
— Jack Canfield, Mark Victor Hansen and Les Hewitt

It's Not Working Brother John
— John Avanzini

Battlefield Of the Mind
— Joyce Meyer

What It Takes To Be #1
— Vince Lombardi

Now Discover Your Strengths
— Marcus Buckingham & Donald O. Clifton, Ph.D.

Personality Plus
— Florence Littauer

Maximized Manhood
— Edwin L. Cole

Man Of Steel And Velvet
— Aubrey Andelin

Wild At Heart
— John Eldredge

How Faith Works
— Fredrick K.C. Price, DD

Hung By The Tongue
— Francis P. Martin

The Dream Giver
— Bruce Wilkinson

Point Man
— Steve Farrar

The Five Love Languages
— Gary Chapman

The Millionaire Mentor
— Greg S. Reid

People Skills
— Dexter Yager

The Winners Edge
— Denis Waitley

The Psychology Of Winning
— Denis Waitley

About the Author

Sean J. Harris is a former Non Commissioned Officer in the United States Air Force, serving during the Persian Gulf War. He was born in Atlanta, Georgia. He is the second of three children. Sean has an extensive and diverse background in Aerospace Propulsion, Law Enforcement and Real Estate. Sean has always had strong desires and ambitions to benefit and take full advantage of the Free Enterprise System many take for granted in this country. Sean's determination and discipline afforded him an opportunity to start his own business in the real estate industry prior to starting his successful Business Development Firm. Sean has developed one of the most sought after School of Business for Entrepreneurs, Senel Global Business Systems. Sean's accomplishment prepared him to be an excellent student of business development and has developed into one of the country's top leaders in business.

Sean and his beautiful bride Janel wed 1999 in Atlanta, GA. Sean and Janel enjoy the blessings of God as they strive to help as many people as possible, who want to be helped in developing successful businesses of their own to have a better quality of life. Sean and Janel humbly, and unhesitatingly state that they owe all their success to God, and to their business mentors.

Today, business ownership is providing Sean and Janel with what they both desire most, freedom to choose, and to have the time to pursue God's purpose for them on this earth. Their business is their ministry, which allows them to live a purpose- driven life.

www.ingramcontent.com/pod-product-compliance
Lightning Source LLC
Chambersburg PA
CBHW020207200326
41521CB00005BA/285